I WILL FIND THE GOLDEN RIVER

==============================

a novel by Dietz Heller

Order this book online at www.trafford.com
or email orders@trafford.com

Most Trafford titles are also available at major online book retailers.

Printed in Victoria, BC, Canada.

ISBN: 978-1-4269-3084-3 (sc)
ISBN: 978-1-4269-3085-0 (hc)
ISBN: 978-1-4269-3086-7 (e-book)

Library of Congress Control Number: 2010904713

*Our mission is to efficiently provide the world's finest, most comprehensive book publishing
service, enabling every author to experience success. To find out how to publish your book, your
way, and have it available worldwide, visit us online at www.trafford.com*

Trafford rev. 4/19/2010

 www.trafford.com

North America & international
toll-free: 1 888 232 4444 (USA & Canada)
phone: 250 383 6864 ♦ fax: 812 355 4082

FOREWORD

Have you ever had a certain melody going through your head, repeating itself endlessly, like a damaged record, particularly annoying when something happened which required your full attention?

Well, I remember some of those tunes, but particularly a certain South-American hit, called "Yes, we will find the Golden River!", a story of some caballeros in Northern Brazil, who had heard about a river further north, where people had found gold nuggets and emeralds It was a wild and exciting song, talking about free and independent guys, out for adventure and gold and precious stones. That sounded so much better to me than all the endless and stupid Nazi-propaganda and the beating of war drums and their hate press like the "Stuermer" which even to us kids sounded unnecessary and demeaning.

I loved this tune, even if it came on at times when I did not care much to hear it.

I wrote this book to get a lot of things off my mind, and to hopefully show people how life in Nazi Germany really was, written by somebody who was there, in prewar Germany, during the war in her army and afterwards.

My homelife was sad and unhappy. My mother was divorced, and did not receive any great help from her former husband. Then she was tied up in a very questionable relationship with a married man. I could not stand it at home anymore. The only chance I had to was to leave and go into the army. By then the war had started . There was a law saying that you could get your graduation certificate without examination - - if you enlisted in the army. I took that offer and enlisted.

I was very patriotic, but I also knew that something was not right. What was it? How could we declare war on Poland? It sounded like a trumped up deal. Then think of France and England ! The Allies would stick together. And there was Soviet Russia, and there was America!

Even if there are thousands of books written about the Second World War and the Nazis; this is a different approach and shows insights which were only possible to one who really wanted to find out the truth and reality, and who dared his life to do that - and then drew his conclusions.

There is danger, there is death, there is suspense and a lot of action. This is not just an autobiography. It is the story of a few young people before ,during and after the war. We meet Signe, a beautiful Swedish girl, whose family just had moved into our neighborhood in Hamburg,and whom I,Dietz Heller and my friend Wolf Rohrbach admired and "loved".. Distrust and jealousy follow, but then a deep attachment wins .

Particularly, though, it is the story of a bond between the two friends and of their vows not to be buried by the Nazi propaganda and not to commit cruel acts, and their fight to stay free in their minds and ultimately live where they can feel free.

But let me tell you my story.

BOOK ONE

CHAPTER 1

Hamburg Harbor Hospital, 1948

"Doctor Heller! Doctor Heller! Please come right away! Captain Hammer has an attack! It looks pretty bad!"

The nurse had stormed into the library, red faced and out of breath. I flung my book on the table, jumped up and we both ran towards the captain's room.

"Get the crash cart, call Doctor Huffmann!" I shouted as we passed the nurses station.

The captain was sitting upright in his bed, fighting for his breath, his eyes wide open, full of fear. Was this Captain Guenther Hammer, my friend from years ago, the famous U-boat captain from the World War? The perennial sample of neatness and correctness in all situations?

This man's hair was tousled, and I could see heavy perspiration on his forehead. He stared at me with fear and desperation. Suddenly he shook his oxygen mask off and started to stammer in spurts, interrupted by desperate attempts to get air:

"Dietz, that friend of yours, Wolf Rohrbach...I did not send him away so he would die! I tried to get him out of the Commander's reach... He wanted him executed for refusing to shoot at the shipwrecked sailors in their lifeboat. He had knocked down one of the gunners...wrestled the cannon out of the other gunner's hands and emptied the magazine by aiming in some other direction--that was plain subordination. That was mutiny!"

Guenther's voice had turned to a shrill, penetrating whining, and his skin turned almost bluish. One of the nurses placed the oxygen mask on him again. I ordered another nurse to give him a tranquilizer. She was very quick in getting it, compressed his upper arm, not even needing a tourniquet, found a vein and gave him the shot.

But the Captain was relentless. Again he threw the oxygen mask off. He would not let me listen to his chest.

"Dietz, you know that I am Nazi, but I am not a murderer. I did not want the commander to have Wolf shot. I got him transferred . . . I did not want those sailors shot either, but to commit insubordination? I respect him for why he did it, yes, but I don't know, Dietz, I don't know!"

The injection worked fast. He began to relax a little now. He even let the nurse hold the oxygen mask to his face. I sat down on his bed, grabbed his hand.

I knew the Captain well from years ago when we were friends and neighbors.

"Guenther," I urged him, almost begged him, "try to relax. do you have any pain? You don't have to talk."

At the same time I knew very well what had happened. He had a brain tumor that had spread all over his body. Now it apparently had invaded vital centers, and this could be his last moments.

Captain Hammer pushed his oxygen mask off again. His eyes had a look as if he had woken up and did not really know where he was.

"Dietz, what ever happened to us, to me? How did we get into this war? We all believed in Hitler, didn't you too? Have the Nazi's lied so much to us? Year-in, year-out? Was it all wrong? Mom and Dad believed in it, Birgit did, Ossie died for it...Oh God, what happened? All this killing, all this suffering. Why?"

For a moment he was just like the boy many years ago, when he was my closest friend, who had all the innocence a boy of ten years of age...before the Nazi propaganda machine changed him completely as it had done to so many people. They made them into blind followers believing in nothing but Germany's destination to become the leader of the world.

All of a sudden Guenther shot up straight in his bed, pushed the nurse away as she tried to keep the oxygen mask on. He stared at me with an eerie, fierce expression in his eyes, shouting now triumphantly: "Yes, Dietz, I will tell you: Germany will be great again! We will have a new Fuehrer! The navy will be big and mighty! Heil Hitler!"

Then he collapsed completely. His eyes fluttered, his head then sank on his chest. He took one long last breath. I grabbed my stethoscope and put it on his chest. I could not hear any heartbeat. I tried to get a pulse. The hand, which I had held previously to give him comfort, now became lifeless and dropped on the bed sheet. Slowly I let it go.

Captain Guenther Hammer, by best friend from years ago was gone.

Dr. Huffman came. As a junior physician, I had to call the ward physician in any emergency. He listened to his heart too. Nothing. The electrocardiogram showed a straight line. Huffman got up and shook his head. Then he said "Dr. Heller, don't feel bad. We expected this to happen any day now. I am sorry, so sorry. I understand he was a good friend of yours years ago."

"Yes, doctor. Thanks."

I left after a few minutes. I felt some tear drops running down my cheek. I was not ashamed.

Oh, it had been so obvious. That was the Nazis biggest and unforgivable sin, I thought. They had abused youthful enthusiasm and devotion and poisoned the minds of so many young people, filled them with their blown-up ideas of superiority, had given them belief in a mission to improve the world by a way of revenge. At the same time they had been made into slaves serving the leaders. Millions had been killed or maimed. How can they be forgiven?

What a horror it must have been, what desperation, when Guenther saw that it was too late now.

I had trouble concentrating for the rest of the day. Guenther's death scene followed me closely, like a stubborn tailgater whose image appeared in my rearview mirror again and again.

. . .

Later on that night I had gone back to my room at the hospital, where I stayed when I was on call, or when it was too late to go home. There was not much to it: a cot, a desk, a bookcase and a chest of drawers with a telephone on it. I could see the rectangular, bleached places on the walls where pictures had hung. Three years after the end of World War II there still was so much damage all over. This section of the hospital had suffered severely, mainly from water, when firemen tried to control a blazing fire on the east wing.

It was hot in the room. I went to the window and opened it and took a deep breath. Cold, humid air poured in. It was foggy outside and I hardly could see the wall, which I knew surrounded the hospital. Some vague outlines of trees were visible. There was one street lantern whose light was dispersed by the fog droplets into millions of tiny stars that twinkled as they moved up and down and around its bright center.

The air was colder than I had expected. I lit a cigarette, shut the window and went to lie down on my cot. I could not help thinking again about Guenther Hammer's death, his despair, his torture, interwoven with memories of Wolf Rohrbach. I had seen Guenther daily since he was readmitted for "terminal" care.

Doctor Bruett, our chief surgeon, had stated that no surgery could be done since the tumor had already spread all over his body. Some radiation was given, without too much hope. Just to do something.

Guenther had been a very good patient. He never complained. He was aware that he was going to die. He never spoke about the war and his experiences as a very successful U-boat Captain; he never spoke about Wolf Rohrbach except that he told me that they had been on the same U-boat for a while.

No, that is not correct. At one time he mentioned him, blurting out that Wolf openly had refused an order of the Commander ,that he had to be transferred to another boat, that it was a disciplinary transfer. He had not behaved like a real German officer and that he would not be welcomed if he ever came back to Germany. What did that mean? It sounded mysterious to me. Guenther then stopped. He never said another word about it.

I had the feeling that he was all by himself with his thoughts, that by heart he still was the submarine officer, thinking of the great men he had met like Captains Prien or Kretzschmar and other U-boat heroes. He was very polite and cooperative, but also somewhat aloof. After a while I had stopped trying to penetrate this mask. I was too busy.

. . .

Whatever happened I did not know, but it sounded like a typical Wolf Rohrbach "thing", who had shown his guts before. Maybe he stood up against some unfair or maybe cruel action, like he did when as a boy he stopped our group singing an extremely dumb and aggressive Nazi song while foreigners looked on.

This fate of my friend Wolf Rohrbach, though, made me think and kept me awake just as much. He was dead, he was killed after he was transferred to another sub, wasn't he? Sure, that is what Guenther had said, that is what the report had said that their boat was a complete loss. If he were alive he would have written, somehow would have contacted his friends. His parents were killed in an air raid.

I had to get some sleep. Tomorrow was a big day. Dr. Bruett had asked me to be second assistant on a long brain surgery case. I had to be in good shape. Get some sleep! I told myself again and again.

I almost was asleep when I suddenly thought about the "Admiral Doenitz order". I knew a little about it, but I had to check it out to make sure. It instructed the navy not to do any unnecessary or deliberate killing, but also not to engage in any rescue operations of shipwrecked sailors, if that meant danger for their own lives. What had Wolf done? Maybe he stopped useless slaughtering. I did not know, and had no hope of ever finding out.

For a while I listened to the sound of foghorns down in the harbor and further down the river. It must have been a hell of a night there on the river in that thick fog, I thought. The foghorns sounded so pleading and scared. Finally they lulled me to sleep.

. . .

CHAPTER 2

I was off the following afternoon and went home. I lived with my mother and grandmother in a suburb of Hamburg. There had been heavy damage from bombing raids: an oil refinery was close by and the British bombers had tried again and again to hit this complex.

Our house had a long crack from the basement to the roof, but it did not matter too much. The garage, though, had been hit, and my grandmother's Opel car lay buried under rubble. We could not do anything at that time. My grandmother had tried to find workers to clear up the garage, but nobody wanted to work unless he was given money and extra food. We had no food to give away.

Like any owner of a house in acceptable condition, we had to take in a number of people whose houses were bombed-out. At one time, three strange families lived on the fourth and third floor. On our level the big bedroom was occupied by another couple, separated only by a double door from my room. These people naturally were very unhappy. Taking a bath was a great problem (three families on one floor). They fought over the use of the kitchen and toilets. There were quarrels and deep jealousy and envy. The toilets seemed to be being flushed all day long. Our central heating system was out since there was no coal available. They had little stoves for heating or cooking. The stovepipes were led out through the windows. At times they had to shut them down when the wind came from the wrong direction. I felt sorry for my grandmother who owned the house. It never would be the same.

Shortly after I came back from the war, I had fixed up a rarely used glass verandah and made a small study out of it amidst stacks of unused furniture. No, I could not heat it. But it was good for warm days and gave me an illusion of privacy.

. . .

I retreated there again on this sunny November day. I put my feet on the desk and leaned back in my chair and my eyes swept over our backyard and the neighbor's yards.

Our own backyard was okay, but the area where the neighbor's house once had stood was now a heap of rubble and pieces of concrete, collapsed staircases and crumbled bricks. Some strangely shaped metal beams stuck out into the air. How our neighbors ever got out in time, I could not imagine.

The view was the same to the east, where all the other houses had been standing; mountains of rubble, broken and splintered dead trees.

Not even a block to the west I could see Hammer's house. Everything in between was leveled too.

The Kessler house to the north was still standing, but it had long, menacing cracks. All the windows were shored up with plywood or cardboard. I had been over there to see how badly damaged the house actually was. Only the basement was safe, and that's where Mrs. Kessler and her daughter lived, waiting for Mr. Kessler to come back from a POW camp in Russia.

The Koehl's house next to it, though, was essentially undamaged. Mr. Koehl, a very big Nazi, had lost two sons in the infantry. A third one was killed as a pilot in Russia. His oldest son had been an SS physician and was in prison since several months. He was suspected of having participated in certain scientific experiments. He was scheduled for a trial and then would have to go through denazification. We had heard Mr. Koehl saying again and again before the war that sacrifices for the fatherland would have to be made. Losing three sons? I am sure he had not expected that. Had his eldest son been part of the inhuman medical experiments done by the SS? Did Mr. Koehl know about it?

. . .

It took all the guts I could muster to maintain a positive way of thinking and to believe in a future for this city or for Germany altogether. The war had left nothing but ruins, destroyed lives and created millions of unhappy people who now had to fight daily to find food, some ways to earn some money, and somewhere to get some heating material to warm their apartments for at least a few hours a day. It was so difficult to live here where you could not trust anybody, and even now one wrong word could destroy your chances at the medical school or for that matter in any endeavor. People were envious, suspicious. I did not dare to trust anyone--just like in the last years in the Army.

Where were all the Nazis? Nobody seemed to have been involved, and when they could not deny it they either said it was the thing to do, or they had been told to join the Party or else.

I searched my desk drawer where I thought I had stashed away half a cigarette.I had found out that cigarettes helped suppress hunger. That certainly was true. But it did not do anything for the weakness, which came from the perfectly insufficient amount of food, which was available.

I found two half-smoked cigarettes, unfolded the paper and wrapped the tobacco fairly skillfully with some cigarette paper. The result did not look great, but it tasted all right.

As the smoke curled up to the ceiling, I studied the moonscape area of destruction in front and at the side of our house. I almost was getting used to this view. Lately some weeds and bushes had pushed their way through the top of the rubble, providing some cover for the plentiful, big fat rats that were always running around, even in plain daylight.

I glanced again at the yellow walls of Hammer's house, which was standing all by itself, practically undamaged through all the bombings. Wasn't that a cruel joke? The Hammers, who had been the greatest Nazis in the neighborhood and had persuaded quite a few people to join the "Party". And their house was undamaged.

As I reflected on this injustice, I thought I could hear a little voice that said, "You can't change the past. Think of your own future; find your own way, Dietz. That will be your revenge."

The afternoon sun made by eyes squint. Before I turned away, I looked once more at all the destruction. Yes, and at Hammer's house; that's where it all began in 1932-33.

The Hammer's were very enthusiastic about a new polititian named Adolf Hitler. His new Party, the National-socialistic German Workers Party, was the center of most political discussions. The Hammer's just loved their vigorous and aggressive ideas, his faith in Germany and her future. He promised to rebuild the German Army, and he started to talk about revenge for the First World War. He endlessly emphasized his hatred for the Jews, and claimed that they had caused Germany to lose the war. But his belief in Germany and her value made him a very strong power, and soon he emerged as the only man who could bring the nation back to where she had been and restore her greatness.

. . .

CHAPTER 3

Guenther Hammer was their second son, just a few months older than I. We became good friends. We had plenty of time playing together, making endless plans and doing all the things ten year old boys do. I envied Guenther because he was so good at sports, while I was clumsy and awkward. He could have qualified for any track team and was pretty good at the long jump. He had a very big nose--so what. He was my first good friend. He envied me because I made better grades and was supposed to be so smart.

Guenther's older brother Ossie also spent some time with us. He was a good-looking boy with dark hair, just as slender as Guenther. He also had big brown eyes like his brother. He impressed me by saying that he was going to be an infantry officer one of these days. He was just thirteen years old.

He had many books about the military and the first World War, and he let us see them from time to time. A lot was being written about the "100,000 men army" that Germany was allowed to have according to the Treaty of Versailles. Many people thought that was shameful and degrading and many severe fights were fought in the press and also in the Parliament over ways to increase its size. Ossie's standpoint was clear; he saw no reason that we should not have a big army like before the First World War.

He also let us look at some pornographic journals. We were flattered, but did not understand much of what was going on there.

I spent a great deal of time at Hammer's house. In our house we could not make any noise because my mother constantly was giving tutoring lessons. My parents were divorced and my father had remarried and moved to Magdeburg. My mother never had much time for us, so I had no reason to stay home. There was always something going on at the Hammers with their constant stream of friends coming and going.

I could see that the Hammers were very nationalistic and revered the armed forces, were proud of what they thought was the great history of the German Nation. But now, in 1932, something else had become their focus of interest; that Austrian politician Adolf Hitler worked himself into the foreground of their attention. We all agreed that we needed somebody who was going to restore Germany's power and might. But an Austrian? Wasn't there somebody in Germany who could do the job as well? Apparently not.

Even we kids had heard a lot of talk about unemployment, about the threat of the communism, and about all the alleged injustices with which Germany had been treated after the World War. We needed a strong man, a "Fuehrer". A man, who would pull us out of this pitiful and shameful existence. Was Hitler "it"? I myself would rather have seen a general or a member of the imperial family become the new leader.

Guenther dragged me to the radio when Hitler was to be on the air again. The whole Hammer family was crouched around their radio set, eagerly waiting for Hitler to start his speech. Endless military march music came from the radio, until it suddenly stopped and the band intoned the "Badenweiler March", Hitler's signature tune.

Then he started to speak. I was perturbed; Hitler's voice was deep and coarse with a strong Austrian accent, and he was hard to understand. At first he recited endless facts, smothering everybody with them--nobody could check them out that fast. I was growing bored. I started to look around. Maybe there was something else to look at or to read.

Guenther saw that I was getting disinterested. "Hey, Dietz, wait a few minutes until he really gets going. It will be wild."

And so it was. Suddenly Hitler had found his enemies. He began to attack them: the Allies, and the Treaty of Versailles, the Jews and the communists. He became more and more insulting and vicious. Once he had the masses on his side, he worked them into a frenzy. They started to yell "Heil! Heil!" at everything he said. I imagined there was now pandemonium in the hall where he spoke.

He also built up all the qualities of the German people, their willingness to work hard, their efficiency, their plenitude of genius, and talked about our famous cultural heritage, qualifications great enough to make us Germans, and only us, the supreme masters of the world.

By the end he was shouting his sentences. The audience responded in kind, screaming, out-of-control, wanting even more, wanting everything.

The Hammers loved it. Their faces glowed. They looked at each other as if they were saying: yes, he is our man. He will avenge all the injustice that had been done to Germany. Both parents had signed up and were becoming ardent Hitler supporters and admirers.

I had mixed feelings. This man was just too much for me. He was violent. Nobody should adore violence, and there was no need to scream like he did.

But the Hammers must know, I thought. They were all so enthused. I pretended that I was equally impressed, but then hesitated when Mrs. Hammer said with a gleam in her eyes that Hitler was a prophet. A prophet? Prophets usually were dead, weren't they? I did not know for sure. I was not even ten years old.

After months of political wrangling Germany's president, Fieldmarshall von Hindenburg , appointed Hitler to be the new Chancellor. The Nazis held wild celebrations, particularly in Berlin.

But for some reason it did not sound right. Hitler never had won a straight election. Why did Hindenburg then appoint him? Yes, sorry to say, but Hindenburg was blackmailed .He and many other landowner were in a scheme to obtain land in the Eastern provinces taxfree. They started the co-called "Osthilfe" law and tried to push it through. Hitler must have found out about it and threatened to expose Hindenburg and the other Junkers. That would have been the end of most of them.

No, my cousin Andreas had found this out and talked to people about it. Unfortunately he must have told it to the wrong people and they reported it. So, he lost his chance to become an army officer. He decided to leave for South-America and never returned to Germany . .

Almost all of our games had turned into soldier's games. We played war at home, deploying toy tanks or toy warship models. In our backyards, great mock battles took place, and tree forts and porches were being conquered.

At times the whole neighborhood got involved. Once two brothers were warring against each other, each having recruited his own army of friends. The brothers lived on a large estate that had a little lake and a very small island at its center. We were throwing objects across the water.

Somebody started to shoot a BB gun. A boy next to me was hit in his face just below the right eye.

'Fortunately, at this point, the mother of the boys appeared and broke it all up before anybody got hurt seriously.

. . .

For a few weeks I went to meetings of the Pathfinders with my older brother Pat, a group that emphasized a nationalistic viewpoint, self-sufficiency, honor, and religion. They met in a nicely furnished room in the basement of a neighbor's house. All boys were older than I. They wore dark blue shorts and blouses. Most impressive, though, were the Swedish knives in their sheathes, attached to their uniform belts. One of the boys showed me the gleaming, large size blade. Pictures of war heroes decorated the walls. Somebody had contributed a steel helmet from the World War. It hung across the wall opposite the staircase and could not be overlooked.

The boys sold magazines about the World War, printed on excellent paper. Who would spend all that money, I thought. Are we not so poor because of that war?

Pat himself was well liked, but definitely did not belong in this group. He never mentioned that he was interested in a military career, he never looked for a fight.

All the other boys, though, talked about nothing else but war heroes, about generals and their own ambitions to become officers or go into the army somehow.

The leader was a very tall and skinny boy nicknamed "Beanpole" Metzger. He never smiled. The boys respected him and did not mind following his orders. I did not like him at all. He seemed to have no interest in fun, and he scared me somehow.

One of the boys reported with trepidation that his father had let him hold a Lueger pistol--unloaded naturally. Everybody listened with envy. Another boy, named Johannes, got up and put something shiny on his right hand, then made a fist. "You know what this is, don't you?" he said. "Brassknuckles! When you punch somebody with them you can cause a lot of pain."

Beanpole looked at him sternly. "Johannes, that is a forbidden weapon, don't you know? It is against the law to use it!"

"My father got it from his friends in the Nazi Party", Johannes retorted, "They carry brass knuckles all the time. He says they are really good when they have street fights with the communists."

"Johannes, we want to use only honorable weapons, weapons that make us proud, like the Lueger pistol or an army rifle. Put that away. We want to be soldiers and not street fighters."

Johannes glowered at Beanpole and slipped the brassknuckles into his pocket. He did not say one more word all evening.

The group started to sing, first some patriotic songs, then war songs.

Beanpole gave a short speech. "Men, you all know what Germany will demand from us. We have to be prepared for the day she will call us to arms. We will follow the great tradition of the German army, and we will fight for Germany's victory in the time-honored Prussian way. Our life does not belong to us, it belongs to Germany, and we will learn how to sacrifice it for her greatness."

And so on. It sounded scary, not so much because of all the talk of sacrificing their lives, but their determination to do so, apparently without questioning. These boys looked serious and completely dedicated. Don't they have anything else on their mind but war? I wondered.

Then they sang a sad song about the destruction of Russia by the "Red Plague," the communist party. They followed with another song, but this one was fun. It told about a shady character in the forest near Nischnij-Nowgorod, who ran a pub, and cheated his customers by serving them diluted vodka and whiskey and by using fixed dice. Why all this Russian stuff? I asked myself. Do they want to try to conquer her again as they almost had done in 1918?

On weekends the Pathfinders meetings consisted of paramilitary drills, parades and constant attempts to bring the marching speed up to the norm of the German army--about six miles an hour. What nonsense, I thought, we are just kids. We smaller boys had to hang on somehow, even jogging at times. We all soon grew exhausted. But we also noticed the determination of the leader and some of the older boys and we were ashamed to say anything.

I quickly tired of this group. Guenther Hammer had asked me a number of times to join the Jungvolk, a branch of the "Hitler Youth" for younger kids. It was an honor to be asked, so I joined. I had some doubts about the political side of it, but to be with friends was more important.

. . .

My older brother Pat came home one day from school. He clearly showed in his face that he was very mad about something. He slammed the door shut and threw his schoolbooks on the kitchen table where I was sitting with my mother.

"What is the matter, Pat?" my mother asked.

"Have you heard that all the youth groups except the Hitler Youth will be dissolved--like nothing? The Pathfinders, the Stahlhelms, all the religious groups! They all have to go and join the Hitler Youth. What right does Hitler have to do that? That is illegal, that is criminal!"

"Pat, it can't be? Why should they want to do that?" my mother asked.

"I will tell you why", Pat said. "So he can make them all into Nazis and into willing followers of his party, and make all of us into good soldiers for the next war!"

I had to disagree. "Pat, all those splinter groups do not make Germany strong. We have to be united to make Germany invincible again, I think."

"That sounds just like the talk you hear at Hammer's, doesn't it? The Nazis are dangerous! They like to use knives, they beat people up, especially the communists. They have no decency, they are loud and drink beer endlessly. I hate them."

He stepped up to me and looked straight into my eyes.

"If I don't want to be in the Hitler Youth, I shouldn't have to be in the Hitler Youth. Please remember that."

"...and I saw that most of your Pathfinder friends had nothing else on their minds but becoming officers or going into the army. What is the difference?"

Pat could not believe what I had said.

"Dietz, I hope one of these days you will see that what counts is your individual rights and feelings, not a mix of weird and aggressive ideas. You sound like a Nazi boy! You have been at the Hammers too long."

Pat broke the conversation off angrily and stormed out of the room. I was confused and also felt somewhat ashamed without really knowing why. I never had seen my brother being so upset.

My mother did not know whose side she should take. "I am not a political person, sorry, I don't know who is right."

What was going on in the Jungvolk? It was almost the same as the Pathfinders: drills, marching, parades and war games--but this time under a different flag, the Swastika. We had political lectures and readings from Hitler's book "Mein Kampf." On the other hand almost everybody belonged to the "Jungvolk." I met many boys and there was friendship and comradeship.

After a few months, though, I found out that I was bored. I found it so ridiculous to run around there and pretend to be a grown-up warrior. I wanted to get something more out of being in an organization. I heard that there was a branch that taught how to fly a glider plane. That sounded exciting. I transferred to this group.

This way Guenther and I became separated. He continued with his group and became more involved. I had the impression that he was aiming to climb the ladder of ranks and advance as far as he could. Guenther Hammer or not--I had started to go my own way.

. . .

CHAPTER 4

The following summer I applied for a "flying camp", where we would be taught how to fly glider planes: simple, sturdy planes, which were catapulted by a crew and just glided down, the basic step of any glider or soaring flight training. I was happy to meet Richie Gattorna, a classmate of mine, who also had signed up for the camp. He was happiest being around cars and trucks, but now had become interested in flying.

He was full of bounce, almost perpetually in some motion or another, full of life and action. He might have had some hyper-mobility problem. He was constantly moving his hands or his upper body. With his nice smile, his dark hair, which created a lot of attention by the mostly blond North German girls, and his friendly way, he made a lot of friends soon.

Both of us had talked a lot mainly about planes and cars and other technical problems. Both of us also were sure that we would be engineers one of these days.

He was fun to have around, and we managed to stay in the same tent.

There was to be a grand opening of the camp, with a lot of Party officials attending. An over-flight by a few planes of the new Luftwaffe had been announced also. That's what we really were waiting for. Hitler had broken another pact and started to build an airforce. Everybody was proud of him, what a man.

But the planes did not come in time, and finally we were released to our tents.

Then suddenly we heard engine noise coming from the South. Three Arado training planes appeared. They were flying unusually low--and very,

very close to each other. Richie and I stared at them. It could not happen, could it?

Hardly had they flown over the camp when the right plane collided with the middle one. The vertical stabilizers and the rudders interlocked for a few seconds. We heard a dull thud and saw pieces of wood break loose and fly off. The planes pulled apart.

"Richie, for God's sake!" I screamed.

"Let's run, Dietz, come on!"

"Where-to? No, let's first watch!"

"Look, he is turning now!"

The right plane was badly damaged. Only pieces of the tail remained. It suddenly veered to the left again, but under the other planes. We saw the pilot jump out. His parachute did not open.

The pilotless plane now made an unexpected turn to the right and started to dive towards us. The engine had stopped, and we could hear only a whistling sound. We threw ourselves to the ground, covering our heads with our arms, peeking upward in terror.

The plane gained speed and righted itself a little, and then it careened directly over us, so close that we could feel a big gust of wind from it. We heard a tremendous crash and the horrible sound of crunching metal. The plane had hit the hill behind the camp.

No explosion, no fire. We boys started to run towards the crash site.

Suddenly the P.A. system started to sputter, then blared, "Stay away! Stay away from the plane, everybody! It might burn or explode!"

We all stopped. We realized that we really did not know what we were doing. The dark green heap of the broken fuselage and the shattered wings; we better leave it alone.

· · ·

The crash was traumatic enough, but in the afternoon the camp leader gave a short speech, acknowledging that there had been an accident, but saying that we--he called us "men" - - what an honor!--had to go on no matter what. We had to keep on flying, for Germany, for the Nazi Party and for victory.

On the last day of the camp there would be an excursion flight over Hamburg in a trimotor plane, and we would go ahead with it as planned.

I went on to pass my first flight-test and received the much desired blue-white seagull badge, indicating that I had soloed satisfactorily. Birgit Hammer, Guenther's sister, saw it and gazed at me with her big eyes, full of admiration. I was the only twelve year old boy she knew who had flown a glider plane!

. . .

Maybe I was not that tough. A few months later, when we started to train for the next test, I noticed that three glider planes were flying at the same time over an abandoned, fairly small airfield. The gliders were pulled up by motor winches, while in the camp we used crews pulling long catapult lines to get the gliders airborne. No teachers would go up with us, not even for the first few flights. We had to disengage the towing line and then fly S-shaped patterns and turns.

Without having a teacher with me? I thought. No, I did not care for that. I got out of the program. Clearly the new Luftwaffe was behind the program, trying to train many hundreds of future pilots. I quit.

Richie Gattorna called me "chicken". Then he said something that bothered me much. "You know, Dietz, I will go on. I like to fly. Maybe this way I can get into the air force later on. We have no money, no connections. My father works, but he drinks his money away. Why shouldn't I try it with the Luftwaffe paying for my education?" Then he strolled over to a group of other boys, whistling a tune, maybe a little too ostentatiously.

I realized that my situation was not really that much different. I had gone to the flying camp because I wanted to find out about flying, yes, but also--the camp was free. For ten days I would not be a load on my mother. I hated to see her work so hard.

. . .

Something else bothered me. It had started earlier that year, but it also came up in the flying camp, where there was a lot of talk about it: homosexuality. I vaguely knew what it was. For a while the newspapers had been full of it. Hitler supposedly had surprised Ernst Roehm and his Stormtroopers leaders in a hotel in Bavaria. He found some of them in bed with young men. Infuriated, Hitler had dealt out unusually harsh punishment, even had a good number of them shot or incarcerated. Why were there no trials, no legal procedures? German law had made this sexual behavior a serious crime, but had never asked for the death penalty. What was going on? I did not know. Hitler sure seemed to have overreacted. I had to find somebody who could explain all that to me.

"Dietz, don't you see? They are bad!" Pat told me when I finally got to talk to him about the Stormtrooper Affair. "I believe that Ernst Roehm and the Stormtroopers want to displace the army, want to eliminate it. There is a deadly fight going on. And you know what? Hitler took the side of the army, not of his Stormtroopers, he was a traitor to his own comrades. Now the Stormtroopers are nothing anymore, they are disgraced forever because of the homosexuality in their ranks--they were decimated by these actions, their leaders are dead. The army has won, thanks to Hitler's treachery. They are deeply indebted to him."

That was hard to take. I did not even think I could believe it.

I thought all this would not affect us boys at all, and we were not judgmental at all. It was not our problem until I saw the camp leader, a boy of about sixteen years and his adjutant. Both of them lived together in a special tent on top of a little hill in the center of the camp.

The camp leader had beautiful skin and wore a specially tailored uniform and custom-made boots. He used fine white gloves and almost worshipped them by taking them off and putting them on, and doing the same over and over while talking to us on roll call. His voice was slightly nasal. Then he combed his hair again and again. His adjutant seemed to be very shy and gazed at him devotedly. The adjutant, too, had beautiful skin, almost like a girl.

One morning Richie Gattorna and I were trying to subdue our snickering when the leader again performed his glove ritual

"Dietz, I bet he wears those gloves to bed." Richie whispered.

"I would not be surprised if those two get married one of these days!" I replied under my breath.

That was too much for Richie. He burst out in loud laughter. The leader glared at us. "Gattorna! Heller! Three times around the hill! On the double!" He loved to use army language. We ran around the assembled unit and came back out of breath, still grinning at each other. We found all this spicy and funny, but also very remote.

Shortly thereafter, the infamous Nuremberg Laws against the Jews were imposed, not too strictly at first, but gradually more. In 1935 the Nazis declared the Jews unworthy of being German citizens and progressively deprived them of their civil rights. Why did they not fight back? I wondered. Were they guilty of something after all? We did not hear about any serious attempts by Jews all over the world to help them.

I did not know why so many people hated the Jews. Yes, there was always somebody who said that they had killed Jesus Christ, but that was not the fault of the Jews who lived now. Was the reason jealousy? Many Jews held very good positions in medicine, in the arts and in law, and made good money. But why shouldn't they? What was it? Hadn't they fought shoulder to shoulder with the non-Jewish Germans in the World War?

Some of my Jewish classmates disappeared never to return. Reportedly they had gone to England or the United States. Many Jews had to sell their property at ridiculously low prices. Guenther Hammer proudly told me that his father, a lawyer, was very busy handling deals of that sort. Other Jews did fairly well at least for a while. Even the Hammers consulted a certain Dr. Goldberg, when their oldest daughter fell sick. But after a few months, Dr. Goldberg was gone too.

. . .

I did not know what to think. I was terrified: my brother Pat had been struck by some unusual muscular paralysis. He was lying in bed, motionless, not being able to move his arms or legs. He could breathe and talk, though.

I tiptoed further into the room. It was dark since the curtains were drawn.

A doctor had been in earlier. He said that Pat had the same muscular disease that our father had suffered from when he was a teenager. It had something to do with his potassium level and that Pat would outgrow it like our father had done. This was Pat's first attack.

I was amazed how calm Pat was. I would have been screaming, I thought.

"Pat, is there anything I can do for you? Would you like me to bring the radio over here, or get you something to read?"

"No, thanks Dietz. I will be all right, the doctor said, maybe after a day or so. Man, why did this have to happen to me? What if this comes back again and again? I don't know."

He was more desperate than it seemed at first. I did not blame him. This could affect his whole life! He was such a brilliant student, at times he had to read a book only once and could remember most of it, had jumped one class in school because his grades were so excellent--he wanted to become a physician, already had started to read medical books.

Pat was my mother's favorite, no question. If I might have had reason to be jealous of him--he had a sail boat and was a member of a rather exclusive sailing club--I certainly now was thankful that I did not have this strange disease.

I was furious, and I had to find something, somebody to blame. Why did my parents have to get a divorce? Why did nobody ever tell us the true story? Why did my father not help support us? He certainly was badly needed now, as Pat was so sick. No, he did not come.

. . .

CHAPTER 5

One summer the Hammers invited me to spend a week with them at the Baltic Sea, where they rented a few rooms for six weeks every year at the same hotel. The whole family went, including their dog.

We spent most of the day on a sand bank, which we reached over a long jetty. We swam in the clear, only moderately salty water, or played ball or lolled in the sun talking. At times the owner of the hotel let us use his small sailboat.

One afternoon Guenther and I were sitting on the hotel porch, listening to Hubi's records. Hubi was a trim, athletic boy from Munich. He had a great treasure: a record player and plenty of records. It was of the type you had to wind up after every other record. Nevertheless, he played it for hours, and usually a bunch of kids gathered around him.

Guenther was listening too, but none of the records seemed to satisfy him. "Hubi, why do you play all that Latin-American music? What's so great about it? Don't you have any German records?"

Hubi laughed, "Hey, Guenther, I just happen to like these records. Rumbas, carioca, South American beat...that's hot stuff now. Listen to this, it is my favorite!"

This was the first time I heard the song "Golden River". It was a wild, exciting tune. The words were hard to understand, but I figured out that a bunch of adventurers were camping somewhere in Brazil, dreaming about a certain river with big nuggets of gold...and emeralds. They were determined to find it, no matter what. They called themselves Caballeros - horsemen, interested in treasures like gold, but not in fighting wars or killing.

Hubi was completely absorbed by this song, smiling happily, nodding to the rhythm. When the record stopped he came back to reality. "Isn't it exciting and fun? Something different, that's for sure."

"It's all foreign music!" Guenther still was not satisfied.

"So what? It's better than all those endless Strauss waltzes or military marches. Wait a year or so. I bet you will develop a taste for this music too."

He flipped through the stack of records and found a few more. "Listen to this one. It is called 'Wahoo', about going for the big fish! Look here; 'I like bananas because they have no bones'. That is the same type of song, just fun."

Guenther frowned. I could see that he was bored.

But something happened to me. I loved this type of song, especially the one about Brazil with its flavor of adventure and the lure of foreign lands.

Okay, Dietz, I thought, don't get carried away. You are not going to spend your life looking for vanilla trees or hunting precious stones or looking for gold like these guys do. And then wind up in a bar being shot after a quarrel.

But I liked the spirit of adventure, the pride and the love for freedom which emanated from this song; not that stupid adoration for the military, which had spread over Germany, not the stupid adoration of the Nazi Party - - everybody tried to get into it, use it as a stepping stone to some higher position or lucrative job, no, you could not get anywhere without being a member of the Nazi Party.

It was as if a feverish excitement had spread across the country: Hitler, Nazis, Army, now even an Airforce - - -we are going to be so strong! We will be invincible!.

Most of the guys felt that there would be a war in the near future. We listened as the older boys engaged in endless talk about the strength of the British or French army, or how many divisions Germany possibly could come up with in case of war. They knew all about the new tanks and anti-tank weapons. Legend had it that a single German soldier could deal with two or three British or French soldiers, or could take on ten to twenty Russian soldiers. Nobody knew where this idea came from, but most of the boys accepted it as gospel.

Sure, a war might be thrilling and interesting, but it also would be bloody. I was thinking of the many casualties, of the wounded and later on crippled victims, who were left from the World War. What had the World War accomplished? Nothing, but create more problems!

No, I rather would venture to foreign countries, maybe even return as a rich man...that would be much more productive than to throw hand grenades and kill people, just so in twenty-five years my son would have to do the same. And I did not want to obey all those Nazis and believe in their weird ideas of superiority of the German and Nordic race, their sickening nationalism and their hatred of the Jews. I wanted independence and freedom of choice,- - even if I really did not know yet too well what that meant.

A few miles away we could see the village of Laboe and the immense memorial for the naval heroes of the World War. The monument was about three hundred feet high and looked like the bow of a battleship. I wondered how it was possible that so much money could be spent to build this memorial while the country needed money everywhere for many vital programs?

Hubi's record player had attracted a rather large bunch of boys and some girls. Most of them went to the sandbank for the rest of the afternoon. Nobody felt like doing anything, and we all lay down in the warm, white sand.

. . .

"Hey guys! Look at that cloud!" Guenther bolted upright, apparently fascinated by what he saw. "Isn't that strange? It is shaped like a giant letter S!"

I squinted into the sky. A long, narrow, sharply-defined cloud hung there ominously, it's edges painted bright silver from the afternoon sun. Actually it looked like the old Nordic letter "S" with it's sharp edges and straight lines. Rolf Zunger, a boy from Saarbruecken, shot a knowing look at Guenther. "It is exactly like the 'S' they use in 'SS'! It means victory!"

His eyes grew wide, as if he were having a vision. Guenther nodded in agreement beaming happily.

"Rolf, you said it! If that does not mean anything I would not know!"

Did they really think that this was a sign from a different world? I wondered. I wished I could have become so enthused. I felt left out. Maybe they knew more about the war and the future than I. I was too proud to ask.

Heck, it is just a cloud. Don't get carried away, I thought. I looked up at the sky again. Already the strange-looking cloud had taken on a less distinctive outline.

Out on the Bay of Laboe I could hear the PT boats roaring, and their rooster tails shot up in the bright sunlight. There will be war; I felt it now for sure. Maybe I can do something to prepare myself and find a way and a different destination than to lay in a grave, next to my comrades, under a wooden cross with my name and the day I was killed.

. . .

CHAPTER 6

I must have started to think a little more at that time. As much as I wanted to, I could not agree with all this happy acceptance of a coming war. I did not have the facts to contradict the Hammers and the other boys, but I knew that something was not right. Somehow the propaganda was too confusing and did open more questions than it answered. Why should other nations want to be ruled by Germany? Hadn't Austria and Germany started the World War? And they had lost it. Why should they want to start another war? Just for revenge?

I struggled with those questions and so many more. For example, why did my grandmother love Germany so much? Her parents were of French and American heritage, moved to New Orleans and later to New York, where she met her future husband, a German businessman. She moved with him to Hamburg, Germany, while her brothers and her sister stayed in New York. My grandmother kept up close ties with them, though, and visited them every summer.

As unapproachable as she was, I liked my grandmother. It became a routine that I brought her the evening newspaper every day, and I read it in her living room.

There was a mystery around her. But I found out what it was.: two of her sons had been killed in World War 1, and the death of one of them had occurred in a very strange and disturbing way: he was shot by his own comrades, who refused to attack a French position because they knew it would be a disaster since the French troops were far better equipped and overpowering in numbers. But he had been threatened with court-martial if he did not attack regardless. . .His plea for delay of the attack was not accepted by his superior.

I had noticed that my grandmother often cried and left the room when her sons fate was talked about. So, we learned not to mention them any more ....

She had her own idea about Adolf Hitler. She admired him for being a self-made man. In her eyes he was like an American entrepreneur, not relying on heritage, but making his own way. During the time when I thought I believed in the Nazis she let me put up the Swastika flag on the balcony. My mother, though, did not care at all for politics, and never expressed an opinion one way or the other except that she did not like the way the Jews were being treated. But she also refused to discuss why the Jews were persecuted and ousted. She only said "One does not speak about these things...."

That left me very unsatisfied. Was there a big secret surrounding the Jews? Why would the adults not talk about it? What was going on?

My life still revolved around whatever was going on in Hammer's house. For a few weeks they had an English exchange student staying with them. Allan was a fine guy, polite and careful especially when the Hammers bombarded him with their political views. He had a nice way of countering and always said that he would think about what they had told him. It was at times a very awkward situation when they badgered him. I felt sorry for him.

One of the main reasons I liked the Hammers so much was the somewhat fabulous Mrs. Hammer. She had become my idol with her always-positive outlook. I admired her for the way she gave the appearance of a happy wife and mother. She moved around very gracefully and was very slender. I never had seen any women wearing slacks. It took me a little time to get used to that.

At times she reminded me of Amelia Earhart; not stuffy, not sensual or scheming, just vivacious and natural. She loved the Nazi Party with all its growing power and drive and loved the army and navy. She had an idealistic view of the armed forces and said that, "...you boys should look at them with a positive attitude. Just don't get stuck in the miserable part of army life." She also told us, "Nobody has to commit cruelties and brutalities in a war unless he wants to."

This was a strange statement, but I wanted to incorporate it into my mind, and use it as a reminder that we had rights too. What would we be able to do though, if we were forced to commit those acts?

One other statement she made frightened me, because it showed a stoical attitude I did not expect from an intelligent person like her. With a stern expression she said, "I believe there will be war, and I expect one of my sons to be killed or wounded. Every generation has to have a war to weed out the weak ones. The strong ones will survive."

I could not believe what she just had said. How could any mother accept the necessity of war, I wondered. Wouldn't she want to do everything to prevent her children from being killed? Was this an accepted attitude of other women too? I looked at two of her sons who were in the room, but to them this statement of their mother's seemed to be nothing unusual. To my great surprise I did not hear them object, nor did they seem to feel uncomfortable.

. . .

CHAPTER 7

Wherever I turned, my fourteenth year was really tough. As much as I wanted to cooperate with my mother, she now made it really difficult. She enrolled me in the classic branch of our school, where I had to learn more Latin and also take up Greek, which I absolutely hated.

"Why should I learn such a dead language?" I complained. "Even Pat, who is almost a genius, did not have to." She responded with the usual "You are too young to know", and "One of these days you will thank me."

I had to go to the Greek classes. Nobody was taking my side, and even Pat did not understand me. I now would be separated from Guenther Hammer and Richie Gattorna, my two best friends. They went to the other branch of school, where the emphasis was on modern languages, chemistry and physics; subjects I was interested in.

For over five weeks I sat there like a lump refusing to learn even one word of Greek while my classmates learned to read and write the Greek alphabet and had started to translate Homer's "Odyssey." I was waiting for my mother to change her mind and let me switch to the other branch of the school. But she never did, even when Mrs. Hammer came over and pleaded for me.

Nothing seemed to be right. The boy to my left in our classroom was a somewhat difficult character named Heinrich von Ellsleben, the son of the Nazi boss of our county. I had noted a number of times how many members of the low nobility had become leaders in the S.A. or other Nazi organizations. Most of them had been unable to become officers since the army was so greatly restricted in numbers.

Anybody with the name Heinrich would have been called after a short time "Heinz" or "Heini". Not so Heinrich von Ellsleben. He was a haughty boy without any sense of humor, used a lot of Party cliches in his language, and always seemed to be on the prowl to convert us boys to Nazism. Supposedly his father was a good friend of Hitler's and spent a lot of time in Berlin.

Somehow he and I were on opposite courses. It became worse when he joined our unit of the Flying Hitler Youth. In no time he had teamed up with the troop leader and became his best buddy, promising him that his father would help him to advance.

. . .

I have to say that Heinrich built very neat airplane models. He won a few competitions. I had quite some trouble and used too much glue, making the plane heavier than expected. There was a tear in the left wing, which I had to repair. It looked ugly.

As expected, Heinrich came over and looked at it. He grinned maliciously and said, "I hope they don't work like that at Messerschmitt airplane factories."

I had nothing to say and stayed cool.

The following week we had a contest and flew our models, all of the same class. Heinrich and I were in the same group. He looked over to me and said sarcastically, "I hope yours will fly!"

Again I managed to stay cool. We then catapulted our models, trying to out-fly each other as far as distance was concerned.

Heinrich's model shot up high in the air, then lost speed and altitude by nose-diving and stalling. It landed far short of mine.

We repeated the competition twice more, and again my model won. Most of the boys came over and tried to find out what had made the difference. Heinrich did not. I knew I had made a mortal enemy, at least for the time being.

Shortly thereafter, though, Heinrich had a great day. I happened to stand close by when he cornered two class mates. I could not help overhearing what he said:". . . and I was standing on an adjacent platform on Dammtor railroad station. On the next platform was a long train standing, all first class cars. That was unusual. But what was really strange were all these Storm Troopers, standing at 15 feet intervals, facing the train, hands on their back, their sidearms in place, watching the train.

On and off a couple negroes faces appeared at the windows, trying to get a glimpse of the outside, staring at the storm troopers. All windows were closed.

A man behind me said that these negroes were members of the Amwerican Duke Ellington Jazz band, passing through Hamburg on their way to Denmark or some other Scandinavian country.

Was I happy that these "Untermenschen", those niggers were not allowed to even touch German ground or speak with Germans. No, we don't want them over here, not now, not in the future."

Woessner was angry and upset. He stammered something like " they are human beings too, even if they are black. . . " Heinrich just grinned and said to Woessner: "You talk too much like a minister's son. You have to learn a lot, man." Then he padded both on their shoulders and left, looking for some other boys to tell them his story.

Woessner had gotten red in his face. He looked at Heinrich as if he was going to kill him. Then he spat on the ground and turned away from Heinrich.

. . .

After about five weeks of passive resistance I decided that I might do some harm to my mother's reputation as a tutor; so I gave in and started to catch up with my Greek. I had to be with all those stuffy boys, who wanted to be teachers or ministers or go into medicine. Fortunately there were a few boys I considered "normal", who hated Greek as much as I did. There was Nolle, Kurt Vogel and "Bubi" Woessner, and later on Wolf Rohrbach. They were levelheaded and we soon formed our own little clique.

I hate to say that I never quite forgave my mother for her adamant attitude, and I lost interest in school.

. . .

I wanted my mother to have some male friends so she would be happier. She did have some on and off, but the men turned out to be either too young or not wanting to marry her. I guess she finally accepted the fact that no one would marry a divorcee with two teenage sons.

One of her students, a teacher himself who wanted to advance and add English to his repertoire, became her steady friend and lover. He was married and had two daughters.

He visited twice a week, and my mother also saw him in his studio regularly. Manfred Hansen was his name. He also was an artist, very good at making prints the old-fashioned way by producing copper plates and then hand-printing them. He liked to call himself "Vinci", after Leonardo da Vinci.

Their affair was hard for me to accept. But it was even worse when both of them started to take weekend hiking trips together. He left his wife behind. I also was left at home alone-- my brother had gone to Freiburg to study medicine. Vinci's wife had a hip disease and could not walk well. I felt even worse when my mother and Vinci walked through the neighborhood arm-in-arm like newlyweds. Once, when I visited his studio, I saw a charcoal drawing showing my mother's nude back. After a while it made me sick to see him coming, always with an expression of guilt or sheepishness. I hated Vinci and was sorry that my mother could not find a stronger, more positive man instead of this...whimp.

Eventually I blew my top, saying that it was not right that he was cheating on his wife so obviously and with such cowardice. Why did he not get a divorce from his wife and marry my mother? She got mad, but did not answer. She had developed a habit of not answering problematic questions; she just stayed silent and left the room. I could not do anything about it.

. . .

The next year was better. We visited my brother Pat in Freiburg and met his friends. They were different, were talkative and discussed all possible subjects. Rudi was a lanky boy, with horn-rimmed glasses. He impressed me with his love for literature, especially English and American, and for the first time I heard about authors like Faulkner and Hemingway.

Rudi also played the guitar and loved to sing American songs like "Dinah", "Honeysuckle Rose" and "Penny Serenade".

These songs and books were a great revelation to me. There is a future, I thought. There is life in this, there is feeling and thinking. This was a thousand times better than Goethe or Schiller and the other German poets, who seemed to me calcified inhabitants of an artificial world. I wished I knew more English, but instead I knew a lot of useless Greek.

Pat and Rudi introduced me to Ulla, a friend of theirs. Her dark hair contrasted well with her light skin. Her face was almost angelic, but she herself was pleasantly down to earth, talked easily with everybody. Ulla had a way of becoming the center of attraction whenever she was around. Everyone seemed to want to be at his best around her, and conversation flowed easily. I was immediately attracted to her and could not deny that her perfectly well-shaped legs excited me.

Ulla said that she was going to study medicine. Why did I have to blush, though, whenever she spoke to me? Dietz, admit it; you have started to dream of her. She definitely had opened the door for me to the world of desirable and admirable girls...for the time being so far out of reach.

. . .

After my mother and I returned home and I went back to school I realized how unsatisfied I actually was. School was boring and frustrating. And I still hated Greek. I started to think that maybe school was not everything, and that maybe Guenther was right spending most of his time in the Hitler Youth. I doubted that, but I started to look around.

Adolf Hitler was coming to town to christen a new battleship. Since Guenther had gone with his Hitler Youth comrades, I decided to go on my own. I wanted to find out whether this man really had what they called "magic" that made people scream and immediately become enthusiastic followers for life. I was aware that I could be hooked too, but so what? I had to know one way or the other.

I found a fairly good place on a grassy knoll. It extended to both sides of the road that led from the high land down to the harbor. Thousands of people were milling around, talking excitedly in anticipation.

Two police officers on their brand-new BMW motorcycles came rolling slowly down the street, followed by a few cars. The crowd became very quiet. Then I could hear a roaring sound coming from the high ground, where we expected Hitler to come from. It grew louder and louder. Soon we could hear clearly that everyone was screaming "Heil! Heil!"

A big black Mercedes appeared slowly around the bend of the road. Adolf Hitler was standing in it, with his right arm raised forward. He did not look right or left.

That was it? Why did all those people scream? I was not enthused and did not feel like screaming. I thought this man looked stern and...dull. What a disappointment. No magic, no excitement whatsoever, at least not for me.

Actually I was more excited seeing the brand-new BMW motorcycles driven by the police officers. There were more cars with high officials. They progressed slowly down the long hill and then made a turn to the right toward the tunnel, which led them across to the other side of the river where the shipyards were.

. . .

The Hammers had given me free access to their house, they even gave me a house key. I could come over any time, read or use their record player whether Guenther was there or not. One day I was sitting in their living room, reading "Motor and Sport", a periodical about cars and especially car races. In the adjacent room Mr. Hammer was dictating to his secretary as he did frequently on weekends. His voice though was muffled, but somehow I could hear every word the secretary said. Suddenly her voice became very loud. "You cannot do this to all those people, Mr. Hammer!"

I only could hear some mumbling when he apparently then tried to convince her of the necessity of his actions. But then I heard her stammer "The Jews are human people too! A lot of them have fought in the World War together with you, next to you. You cannot take their property away like that. Why should they be punished? What for?"

Again I could not hear what he said, but he spoke for quite some time.

Suddenly she got up and ran out of the room, crying. I had a glimpse of her holding her handkerchief in front of her face, which was beet red. Fortunately she did not see me.

There had been some talk, but now I knew for sure that Mr. Hammer was expropriating Jewish property illegally. I did not know why the secretary did not quit her job, especially since she had all reason to do so; her sister's husband, a Jewish lawyer, had been told to leave the country as soon as possible. He was preparing himself to immigrate to South Africa in the next few weeks.

I now saw clearly that I had to learn to stay away from the Hammers. Whatever was going on there, this was not my line.

A few weeks later I heard that Mrs. Hammer asked her husband for a divorce. She had found out that he had a mistress in Berlin.

I felt that the world of the Hammers was shattered once and for all.

. . .

CHAPTER 8

"Have you met the new guy yet?" My friend Nolle came up to me just before classes. "He seems to be very sharp, is good in sports..."

A transfer was always a welcome interruption - particularly during the Greek lesson - since usually half an hour or so was lost with introductions and the necessary paperwork.

His name was Wolf Rohrbach. He was given a seat next to me. After class we talked and we hit it off immediately. His father was an executive in one of the major radio manufacturing companies. He was transferred back to Germany from his assignment in Singapore.

I thought Wolf was great. He brought with him the aura of mysterious far-away countries, different cultures, and showed refined English manners, which I loved to observe. It became clear very quickly that he was a boy who wanted to live and not only achieve satisfactory grades in school. He loved life and was interested in a lot of things, especially sports. Despite his upbringing in the British sphere, he was not at all reserved or standoffish.

The Rohrbachs moved to a house not far away from mine. We soon became good friends, especially after I found out that Wolf hated Greek almost as much as I did, and he too could not understand why he had to learn it. Wolf was athletic-looking and seemed to be strong. He had rich, dark hair. I noticed his particular gait, which reminded me of a panther on the prowl; to me this stride said, "Don't try to fool me." I thought that he was far ahead of my dreamy ways. I liked him because he was outspoken and fair-minded.

We began to do some of our homework together and spent more and more time either at his house or ours. Although both of us were still angry that we had to learn Greek, we decided there was no point in nurturing our self-pity any longer. Instead, both of us started to concentrate on the hated subject, and after a while we earned acceptable grades.

The first time I visited Wolf's house I was greatly intrigued by the plenitude of expensive Chinese furniture - beautifully carved chairs, tables, and end tables, made of rich, dark wood. Silk prints hung on the walls, showing strange flowers and exotic birds. On an ebony chest stood a bust of Buddha. I saw large vases with intricate patterns, and a few vases made of jade.

"You know Dietz, I like it in the Far East," Wolf said. "I would not mind going back there any time. We had a beautiful, big house near Singapore. We had a chauffeur, several other servants - nothing wrong with that. Everybody spoke English. I learned a little Malaysian, some Chinese and a few words of Pidgin English."

"Then, why did you leave?"

"I guess my Mom was homesick, and they wanted to have me educated in Germany. Also, business was good in Germany and my father was offered an excellent position here in Hamburg."

A few weeks after Wolf's arrival the class went on a boat tour through Hamburg Harbor. Choppy waves from tugboats and many other vessels made it a rough trip. On the boat also were about ten other sightseers. Some of them looked like foreigners. I heard them speak English and Wolf told me that he heard that they were from Liverpool.

After a while we started to sing. We sang Nazi songs because everybody knew them, and we had not learned anything else for years. Some boys started a new, very aggressive song with the refrain, "Today Germany is ours, and tomorrow it will be the whole world!" The lyrics were dumb and arrogant, although the tune was catchy. I did not feel happy. Of all songs, this one was stupid and offensive.

Wolf looked around, incredulously, looked at me in a questioning way. I realized that he probably never had heard this song before, while we all, unfortunately, had gotten used to it.

Wolf stood up, red in his face. "Stop that song! It is dangerous and stupid! I hope you don't mean what it says!"

The singing died down. Some boys were angry with Wolf, others snickered. For a few moments everybody shifted about uncomfortably, looking at each other, not really knowing what to think. Then some of them started another song about the beautiful daughter of a forester. Her name was Erika and all the men were dreaming of her. Other boys joined in and finally everybody sang.

Some of the boys, though, still looked at Wolf, shaking their heads. Wasn't it fun to show off in front of the foreigners?

Later on, when we were on the bus again, Wolf came to me. "You know, Dietz, I am not so sure that the English people did not hear and understand that song about the Germans wanting to conquer the world. I am sure they would not like it if they could have understood all the words. Would you want to hear a song like that when you were visiting in Italy, or Russia, or some other country?"

"I agree totally. Wolf. By the way, you were courageous standing up like that", I said.

The next morning in school, Mr. Prinzhorn was furious. Prinzhorn had earned our respect because he taught very well and was stimulating. Although his vision was badly impaired - he had to bring his book almost up to his nose, even with the strongest corrective glasses - we did not treat him the usual way. We refrained from jeering or throwing objects through the air like paper airplanes or rags used to clean the blackboard.

"Boys, you sang an outright foolish and dangerous song yesterday. Just imagine that those English people understood the words. They will hate us and fear us even more. I don't want to hear that song ever again. As a matter of fact, you should talk with your Hitler Youth leaders and ban it! By the way, Rohrbach, I think you were very courageous!"

I had a great admiration for Prinzhorn. German was my favorite subject.

But a new teacher, a veteran of the World War, who had lost a leg in the battle of Sommes, soon replaced him. He turned out to be an ardent Nazi. All he talked about was the old Germanic tribes and Siegfried, Brunhilde and Hagen, the world of Richard Wagner's operas, so greatly loved by Adolf Hitler.

He glorified their life with endless tales of beer or "Met" drinking heroes. And we knew that they all wound up killing each other or being killed, dying a bloody death on a battlefield. No, thank you, Mr. Reinicke.

One day Wolf asked me what at first seemed to be a very dumb question. "What are you doing at your meetings in the Hitleryouth? Besides building model airplanes or flying gliders, I mean. What are the others doing who do not build airplanes? Are you learning anything? You know, when I was with the Boy Scouts in Singapore, we had lectures, some teaching movies, and we learned how to build tents and make a campfire.

We had lessons in First Aid. Even our parents came to teach us at times. All the teaching people were adults."

I felt like a fool. What were we learning? Songs, yes, about the great Germany, and war songs. Supposedly youth should teach youth, that's what they constantly were saying. They were teaching us about Germany, about wanting to be a hero, willing to die for the fatherland. I did not learn anything worthwhile. I realized that I was only putting in my hours since I had stopped flying. It had become so easy. Wasn't that a waste of my time? I did it because by now you had to belong to one branch or the other of the Hitler Youth. There was no way out. And a part of me supported this idea. What is goingn on?

Wolf continued, not really having waited for a clear answer from me. "Why does everybody have to belong to the Hitler Youth, one way or the other? If I did not want to I shouldn't have to. I bet you have already settled for being a member of some Nazi organization for the rest of your life. Man, start thinking!"

"Wolf, we all have to be in something, to help build up a new Germany."

I stopped. I did not sound right, it did not ring true. I saw myself in a flash: a member of the Hitler Youth, I was going to the meetings, but my mind was not with it anymore. Would we have to go - forever? Maybe until we were sixty-five? Or, until Germany was great and strong? I did not know.

Ultimately even Wolf had to sign up. He joined the navy branch of the Hitler Youth, spending most of his time sitting around on sailboats, occasionally sailing on the river. At least they taught him seamanship.

. . .

The Nazi Party increasingly tried to become the deciding judge and supervisor of whatever we did. If you forgot or refused to write "Heil Hitler" at the end of an application or any formal letter, you could be sure that it would not be answered. Even bills from certain stores were signed "Mit deutschem Gruss(with German greetings)" or "Heil Hitler". Why did the adults tolerate this nonsense? The Nazis wanted the nation to be unified under Hitler. He was supposed to be the only one who could bring us back to power and strength and importance. Idealistic as we boys were, we could not see reason enough to fight all the intrusion into our life. And then it was too late.

Almost every month seemed to hold another bad surprise. We learned that about three miles away in an old, beautiful mansion along the Elbe river the SS had started a "Lebensborn," which meant something like "spring of life." Here SS men and willing maidens would meet and sleep together - no marriage license required - in order to create future soldiers and fighters for the nation. The babies would be taken care of and educated by the Party. When they were ready the SS or some other organization would cash them in and make good soldiers out of them.

Wolf and I first laughed about this crazy, insane idea. Then we became concerned. Would we want to be born into this world only to become cannon fodder for a glorious Germany?

We heard persistent rumors about a hospital in Altona where under the auspices of a world-renowned obstetrician - the father of a friend of mine - mass sterilization of gypsies was performed against their will.

This was bad. No adults objected openly. The churches remained silent too. No parent group spoke up. This was something that did not let us go. Would I want to have my wife sterilized against her will? No.

What was going on?

. . .

One good and more cheerful development helped our mood: jazz and big band music had broken across all borders. Hamburg had a free port and despite import restrictions for practically everything we could get records from America and England.

This was something new and exciting: Wolf and I listened to Benny Goodman, Artie Shaw and Louis Armstrong, later on to Glenn Miller and many other bands. We whistled their tunes, and we enjoyed the crazy songs like the "Flat Foot Floogie with the floy-floy." This was now our music, and there was great competition at parties who had the newest foreign record.

Nobody could stop us. We had our favorite tunes. Wolf just loved "Jeepers Creepers" and at times drove me wild, whistling or singing it so many times. My favorite tune was the "Tiger rag", and I probably did the same to him.

It did not take long until the Nazis counteracted. They called this "Negro music" or "Jewish music", and labeled it as "Un-German." I had listened to it religiously on our small radio set, but now since jazz was banned from all German radio stations within the reach of our radio, only large and expensive radio sets could pick up Radio Luxembourg or London, where they played it. I could not pick up these stations. But Wolf with his large radio set even found a CBS short wave station in New York, which closed off at about 7:30 a.m. They played a lot of jazz. The announcer always ended saying, "Good night, everybody, and don't forget to kiss your wife."

From now on Wolf and I met every morning at his house to hear a few minutes of this broadcast, before we went to school.

CBS in New York - just think of that.

. . .

By now I started to realize that my friendship with Wolf was different from any others I had. This boy was a wake-up call, a challenge. We were able to talk about political issues and we felt the same about all the nonsense that the Nazis were introducing. The hardest problem for me was to actually see that these stupid ideas were becoming a reality, that all this was not a dream, like the song about Germany going to conquer the world. Those guys did not mean that verbally, or did they? There were people behind these ideas who totally believed in them, and who wanted to make them permanent and change forcefully our lives and our thinking.

When Wolf had said that I already sounded "like a permanent Nazi follower", he had opened my eyes, even if it had hurt me. He had challenged me, and I had become restless. He had done me a great favor, probably without even knowing it.

It was either at our house or at Wolf's place that we got together to do our homework. Wolf realized that in our house the doorbell rang about every hour and a student of my mother's had to be let in. Usually I answered the door and sent them to the lecture room.

Wolf laughed. "Dietz, you have it made! Look at all these girls, day in, day out! You can take your pick!"

I smiled, but I really had not thought of it that way. Some girls were okay: there also were quite a few boys taking tutoring lessons. To me the constant flow of students was a nuisance and I felt like a doorman.

But one day a new girl started to come. She definitely did it to me. Her name was Signe Dahlgreen. Her family had come from Sweden and recently moved into our neighborhood. She took lessons to improve her German and generally to adapt to the school system.

Signe had long, stunning flaxen hair that hung smoothly down her neck and back. Her voice was soft and melodic, and she always had a friendly smile. Her face was beautiful and her lips were...attractive. Somehow the word "classic" came to my mind, probably inspired by her even and smooth movements and her attitude which showed a lot of modesty and restraint. I wished she would come every day.

Signe, what a name. It was so much more exciting and intriguing than all those Gerda's and Inge's and Ursula's. How could I get to know her better?

I was not interested in pointing her out to Wolf. In my imagination I had already taken possession of her. I knew he probably would meet her too, since she lived a few houses down the street from Wolf. But why should I invite trouble? I knew he was fairly lucky with girls.

A few days later I had the strange but pleasant feeling that this would be a lucky day. First I received honors for my term paper on which I had worked for quite a few weeks. Then my father sent us a large smoked ham. That was very unusual since he never called or sent presents to us.

The best thing, though, was that I knew Signe would come for her lesson in the later afternoon. My feelings for her had steadily increased. When I opened the door for her I asked whether she would like to play Ping-Pong with me when she was done. She smiled her beautiful smile.

"Sure, Dietz, that will be fine. I'll see you later."

We had fun playing table tennis. Afterwards we sat down to talk. Signe said that she liked it in Sweden, but also that she started to enjoy it here in Hamburg. School was okay, but she preferred the coed system in her school in Stockholm; it was more fun. She pitied her classmates here who had to go almost everyday for some meeting or some other duties for the "Bund Deutscher Maedchen," which was just like the Hitler Youth. She smiled when she said that all of them had started to look alike in their uniform.

"What else are they doing? They don't have any fun, they march and carry those flags. They don't care for nice dresses and are forbidden to use lipstick - it would be Un-German! They don't talk about boys. All they want to have is a large family, with plenty of boys to serve the 'Reich'!"

"Yes," I answered, "there are so many girls like that. They want six children or more."

"What a life. In Sweden you could talk and do things with the boys. We went horseback riding or swimming, and did other things with them. Yes, I started to do some dating, but we never did...you know what."

It was strange. Despite all the hormonal pressure I felt different in her presence; we had a clean, enjoyable relationship, built on my admiration of her.

"Let us get together again, Signe." I said. "We will find something interesting to do."

"It was fun, Dietz. See you." I let her out and closed the door.

. . .

CHAPTER 9

We were smoking. Wolf and I had taken a liking to the new American tobacco brand introduced recently by the "Gold Dollar" cigarettes with its fruitful and strong aroma. We switched from the oriental tobacco cigarettes whenever we could, but neither one of us smoked much. It also cost money.

We were supposed to do homework, sitting in front of Wolf's huge Blaupunkt radio. Somehow, though, neither one of us could concentrate. Wolf put his pen down and looked at me.

"Dietz, tell me what you know about the SS."

I must have looked perplexed. I was no expert in this matter.

"What do you mean, Wolf? You know that the SS is the elite group of the Party, that it is hard to get in. They have out-maneuvered the Storm Troopers completely. There are a lot of other rumors about the SS, and whatever I tell you is hearsay."

"Well, go on. Tell me what you know."

"SS, the Gestapo and some Security forces, all seem to be under the command of Himmler. They scare me with their black uniforms and the side arms bearing the motto "Blood and Honor" and their secrecy about their actions. They love power in any possible form. There are so many rumors..."

"Do you know anything specific they are doing?"

"I know that they are involved in running the concentration camps. That's about all I know."

Wolf's small room by now was filled with smoke. Wolf opened the window. Then he continued.

"Your grandmother, wasn't she born in America? What does she think about all these problems?"

"I don't know. In our house we never discuss anything. And she lives alone upstairs."

"I thought she might be offended by some of the things Hitler and the Nazis are doing. Never mind..."

It was as if a dentist had touched a nerve with his drill. Wolf again had found a very sensitive spot, maybe unknowingly. Was I that insensate to all these problems? Did he think my grandmother was so stoical that she did not care what happened in Germany?

Wolf continued, apparently not aware that he had shaken me. Like the other day, when he had called me a "perennial Nazi follower."

"All these questions came up a few days ago when a good friend of my father visited us. He is British. He told us a few things I did not know anything about, for instance that Hitler is a carbon copy of Mussolini, who successfully had started his Fascist Party and later established himself as a political force. Hitler tried the same, but failed miserably and had to go to jail. Yes, and also; are you aware that Hitler never won a direct victory in any national election? That he was made Chancellor by Hindenburg..."

"...because Hitler threatened to reveal certain manipulations his son Oscar had done, cheating on taxes for large real estate transfers?" I interrupted Wolf. "Yes, it is plainly rotten."

Wolf continued after having picked up a copy of the London Times.

"Look at this, Dietz. Here it says that the new battleship Bismarck actually is 20,000 tons heavier than it was allowed to be. Their guns are heavier too than they were supposed to be. Don't they know that the British have an excellent spy network? They know about any weapon we have or which we might be developing. They also know about the Russians building innumerable tanks east of the Ural mountains.

The "Times" said that England would not mind having a fairly strong Germany so they can keep the Russians from getting into Europe.

I wish I could have heard more of these stories, but my father made me go up to my room."

It was all so complicated, and actually frightening. Both of us felt talked out and tired. We had no luck with our homework and decided that we somehow had to finish it later at home.

I opened the front door at home. I heard my grandmother and my mother arguing loudly, upstairs. They spoke English and then French when they had heard me come in. This occurred every so often and usually was terminated by my mother racing down the stairs. No, I never was told what the fighting was about. I had to draw my own conclusions, and one of them was that neither one was ever happy.

. . .

When Wolf came to my house one afternoon grinning broadly, I knew he had some interesting news.

"Dietz, I have something for you. We just picked it up from BBC London. It is about Joseph Goebbels, the propaganda minister, who is a nymphomaniac as you know. He likes to chase movie stars, and at a big party he pestered actress Olga Tschechova. When he started to grab her she took a big swing and slapped him in his face, really hard. That is great! I bet you never will read about this in any German newspaper! They told Hitler about it and did he ever chew Goebbels out.

The other report is even worse. BBC said that Hitler can not hold his wind and repeatedly has embarrassed foreign dignitaries when he let go at the wrong moment."

Both of us laughed hysterically. I could not stop myself from saying, "that deflates...I guess both of them pretty well."

We also knew about the sordid affair between Hitler and his niece Gela, that ended in the tragic death of the girl. Hitler a God-sent man? Never!

.

Despite everything, Hitler's star kept on climbing. He freed the Rhineland, later on annexed Austria, went into Czechoslovakia, built up his army more and more and increased the pressure on the Jews.

"Fuehrer, befehl! Wir folgen Dir!"

"Leader, we will follow your command!"the people sang

"Ein Reich, ein Volk, ein Fuehrer!"

"One empire, one people, one leader!"

All these messages were drummed into our minds day after day by the press, by radio and in the movies, and--in school.

The generals knew well that the army was not ready for war. They lacked men, equipment, tanks, planes and especially oil. But how could they resist the idea of a war that would bring them honor, decorations and chances of unheard dimensions?

. . .

It did happen. Wolf had met Signe. They went out a few times together without my knowing at first. They played tennis and she watched him play field hockey. I was angry and jealous. I had no right to be possessive, and I did not want to be, but I thought Wolf could have told me about it. I saw a rift developing.

The next time we got together I asked him about it. I managed to remain cool, but inwards I was seething.

"Wolf, what about you seeing Signe...did you not know that I--"

"Yes, I knew, Signe told me. But this is a free world, isn't it? I can see her, why not?"

This was the first time I had seen him angry. Maybe he thought I was a really petty guy. Maybe I was.

"Wolf, maybe it is too much to ask from you. I thought if it would have been me I would have told you about it, for the sake of our friendship."

I was mad and broke off the meeting after a short while. The heck with him. I was not going to give up on Signe. Maybe she liked to be courted by several guys. I had to find something I could offer her, something Wolf did not have. Then I got a good idea.

Pat had left the motorcycle at home when he went to college in Freiburg. It was not in the best condition and needed a tune-up, but it would do. I was going to take a ride with Signe down the river to an area where I knew was a beach where you could walk as far as you wanted. It was too cold to go swimming now, and hardly anybody would go swimming in the Elbe River because it was so polluted.

Signe was all for it. We drove west on the Elbchaussee, a beautiful road with many mansions overlooking the river. The late summer air was pleasantly warm and the sun was bright.

We walked on the beach and watched the little waves playing with the sand, rolling forth and back.

Finally we came to a few rocks and sat down and looked across the wide river into the afternoon sun. A large fishing trawler steamed up the stream, hurrying to unload its catch, throwing big waves from the bow.

She let me kiss her. She was so soft and pliable, and so relaxed. Her lips felt sweet and warm. Suddenly she slipped a little and held on to me, inadvertently touching me fairly low on my body. She must have noticed my excitement, but she left her hand there.

Signe looked up to me with a slight expression of astonishment. Then she said slowly, "Dietz, not now, not yet. It is wonderful to be with you here, but I do not want--more than that. Let's wait for later. I know it will be harder for you than for me, but I am not ready yet." Again the mysterious power I had noticed before took over. As eager as I was she could divert any aggressive thoughts with a vision of a future when everything would be the way we wanted it to be.

"Signe, you are a wonderful girl. I think you are worthwhile waiting for. I love you."

"Dietz, I love you too."

On the way back, actually for the next few days, I had a marvelous feeling within myself. At this time the thought that Wolf might be lurking in the background, waiting to get his turn, did not bother me. I knew I was in love, and she had said that she was in love too.

. . .

I ran into Guenther Hammer in front of our house. I had not seen him for a long time. I had passed him here and there, but he always was in Hitler Youth uniform on a way to some meeting. I heard that he had been given a free trip to the Party Congress in Nuremberg the previous fall. He still liked to talk about it.

"Dietz, you would not believe how fantastic it was!" he said with his face aglow with memories. "All these SA and SS men, thousands and thousands of other party members were in a very large, brand-new stadium. The meeting was long and it became dark. Hitler was speaking, and suddenly hundreds of flak searchlights blazed on, shooting straight up into the sky. We were in a giant cathedral of light. People screamed in excitement. Then they rolled wheels with burning swastikas from a hills - I could have died, it just was like a religious experience!"

"Yes, I heard about it and saw the newsreels. It must have been something." I was not enthusiastic. This event had been blatant theatrics, obviously designed to impress the people. "Show business!" as my brother Pat had said. While I had felt embarrassed by this publicity stunt, he had said outright that he hated it.

The propaganda mill of the Nazi Party was turning out article after article, promising the Germans a wonderful future, saying that the Germans were the only people in the world capable of living up to their destiny; being the leader of the world. The French were weak and spoiled, the Poles and Russians were of an inferior breed that never would match our German, Nordic blood. America was not interested in war or military matters, and England was so small with their insignificant army and had nothing but their navy.

From now on foreign newspapers were forbidden, and you could be punished if you were caught listening to foreign radio stations. Some neighbors appointed themselves to be watchdogs and reported gleefully the slightest transgressions against the Nazi ideology.

During the next year, 1939, the mood went back and forth between peace and making war. The Hamburg area became the place for extensive maneuvers with troops and equipment filling the streets of our suburb, with flak cannons on almost every street corner, and dive-bombers screaming over our heads. Bahrenfeld airport was reactivated and some fighter squadrons were stationed there. We watched as the pilots revved up their engines and the props blasted the grass behind the planes down to the ground. More and more men volunteered for the armed services. Now it was obvious that something was going to happen.

In late August 1939, everything calmed down. But this lasted only for a few days. Suddenly everything changed when some "Polish" commandos broke into a Silesian radio station - supposedly - seized it and killed several people. Now the press had their victims, and it screamed and howled, "Despicable Poles! Warmongers! We will get our revenge!"

On September 1st 1939, Germany attacked Poland.

. . .

CHAPTER 10

I saw the newsreels a few days later. Hitler was declaring war on Poland, speaking from the podium of a provisional Reichstag building. He did not wear his brown-shirt Nazi uniform, no, he wore a field-gray army uniform, his Iron Cross sparkling. The hall was filled with officers in army, navy and air force uniforms. You could see quite a few older generals from the First World War. They had polished their medals so that they were shining brightly. Everybody smiled in deep satisfaction.

Clearly this was the day of the armed forces. It was more important to belong to them than being a member of the Nazi Party. Where were SA or SS uniforms. Yes, there were some.

Hitler again was what he had been 25 years ago; a servant of the military, even if he now was their commander. He had done what the armament industry had paid him for. He had built up a tremendous war machine so that their factories would prosper and make millions and millions on profits. His face glowed with pride. The frenetic applause of all the military men made me shiver.

. . .

Was all this a bad dream? How could this have happened? Germany had started it. Nobody else.

The idea of war did not seem to fit into this beautiful September morning. Wolf and I bicycled to school, and at the same time German troops poured into Poland.

Most people were confused and did not know what to think. But it was strangely obvious that certain schoolteachers already were perfectly organized; they knew what to do, had already made plans for juniors and seniors to stay in the school building to act as air raid wardens. Juniors and seniors had to stay in school, sleeping on mattresses already prepared. This was very suspicious to me. Had they known ahead of time when the war would start?

Not one of my classmates said that he hated the Poles, nobody wanted to kill them.

I don't think anybody really grasped the fact that we were at war. It was a little bit like a few years ago, when Joe Louis knocked out Max Schmeling in America; people just would not believe that it happened.

No Polish planes appeared over Hamburg. School had been canceled for the time being. We were sitting around all day long and slept through the night, went home in the morning for breakfast and to shower and shave, and went back to our job.

It did not take long and we met Mr. Zeller, the man in charge of the plumbing and the heating system. He liked to talk to us boys and frequently joined us, usually with a bottle of beer in his hands. Under normal circumstances it would have been more than a sin to have a bottle of beer in a German school. But now it was war.

Mr. Zeller had been in the World War on a battleship and participated in the battle of Juetland. He once gave a description of the battle itself - how they spotted the British ships, how heavy shells came howling and crashed into the sea not far away.

He was against the war, absolutely, even if it did not involve the British and French at this time. But he was fearful that England would live up to her commitment, take Poland's side and get into the war unless the German troops retreated immediately. Whenever we boys talked about this possibility, he became silent and pensive. He actually said, "Boys, let's not even think of England getting into the war. It would just be horrible."

Some of the boys could not keep from asking him why he was so afraid. England was a small country; her army was not that great.

Mr. Zeller rolled his cigar between his lips. He did not look healthy, I guessed he liked beer a lot. Many little blotches marked his face. His eyes were watery.

"Just think of her navy. It is ten times bigger than ours is. They have a good number of battleships, many cruisers, and they have plenty of destroyers. They know what they are doing. The British have kept their empire intact for many, many years. Our navy men themselves have said it would take us five to seven years until we can even think of matching them."

Kurt Vogel, a classmate, was not happy with his statement at all. "Mr. Zeller, we are told that our dive-bombers will destroy their big ships easily, like nothing."

"Don't expect that they can do the whole job. The British air force is not small," he replied. "They have a new fighter plane, the Spitfire, which can take on the dive-bombers easily."

"We have the Messerschmitts, the world's fastest fighter plane!" Nolle was angry. Apparently he did not like Zeller's negative attitude.

Mr. Zeller now was puffing away on his cigar.

"I tell you, it is this way. Whoever starts the shooting will unleash a bunch of furies and will push the sympathy of all neutral nations to the side of the attacked party. England has a lot of friends in the world. They will draw the Canadians into the fight, their Indian troops, and I would not be surprised if they don't manage to get the United States into the whole mess.

What do we have? We will have the Italians with us - but you know the saying that in a war the Italians always wind up on the other side?

We have practically no oil, not enough steel, no natural rubber. The army has the will to fight, and the determination..."

Mr. Zeller took a long sip from his bottle and licked his lips. He also had to wipe his forehead, but he wanted to continue.

"...but we can't again take on the whole world! There are millions and millions of decent German people: did they not see how they were being led towards another war? How the Nazis pounced on them day after day to demand revenge for the wrongs the Allied did to Germany after the World War? How the Nazis kept on saying that the Jews and communists had betrayed them? Did they not see that Hitler built up their self-pity, made them gradually lose their sense of responsibility, made them want nothing but revenge, revenge, revenge?

"You boys may think I am just a dumb handyman, but I recommend to you that you read a lot of history, read about all these things. Germans never really were free, they always were led and manipulated by their kings and dukes. We had to do what we were told to do and usually had no choice. And now the German people have been talked into following a selfish and power-drunk man. You have heard all those fanatics when they scream and scream when he speaks. That's when they gave up their right to determine their own fate."

59

We never had heard anybody talk like this. Nobody would have dared to. Zeller could easily wind up in a concentration camp. And he had thrown quite a few problems at us, problems with which we could not deal at this time.

Mr. Zeller had worked himself into a state of excitement. His skin had turned dark, somewhat livid, and again he had to wipe the perspiration from his forehead. Some of the boys really felt sorry for him, others I looked at were not that much interested or impressed. I guess most of them had to admit that he was serious. All this could not be true, could it?

He continued after a short pause. "What is going to happen after the Western powers kill each other off again? Sure, Russia will roll west with her thousands of tanks. And the Japs? Whatever happened to Hitler's philosophy of the pure, white super race? He would not mingle with the yellow race, would he? Aryans and Japs together?"

There was no way of stopping him. He continued, "But really, besides the Far East, don't you see the direction? Germany attacks Poland, then England will declare war and France won't wait long. Ultimately the war will extend to Russia--Hitler always wanted their land--and maybe then to the United States. It would be the whole mess again, like in 1914. You all have had French lessons, haven't you? You know the saying "deja-vu": it looks as if everything has been here before. Ja, repeat performance! I wish I could laugh, but I don't feel like it. I am too old to be drafted, but you guys, you will have to go. No, it will not work out this time either!"

He got up. Kurt said, "Mister Zeller, there is no war against England and France at this time." Mr. Zeller looked at him with a wistful expression. "I hope it will stay that way, boy, I hope it will." Then he walked away.

Most of us were confused. Maybe the old man did not have any guts or any faith in Germany.

Kurt then said slowly. "I know him, I have met him a few times. He is a friend of my father. They were in Teachers college together. He had to quit because he ran out of money. My father always said he was a brilliant student, who loved French and English. He said it was a shame that he could not become a teacher."

"Man, he is sharp." Wolf added. "He knows his history. I did not expect a janitor to know all this."

The next morning we were sitting on the front steps of the school, doing nothing. I was glad to see Richie again and talk with him. His class also was involved with the air raid warden program. He told me about all the girls he supposedly knew well, and that he had done it with some of them. "You know, they just can't resist my Italian charm" he laughed. I had the feeling from the way he talked that his adventures sounded a little bit too successful.

Klaus had brought a new record by Louis Armstrong called "Shadrack". It was a little strange, but we liked it. More fun though was another record with the song "Ferdinand the Bull."

At about one o'clock Mr. Zeller came storming out of the main door. He saw us hanging around there, threw his cigar away and almost screamed, his face showing nothing but agitation. "Boys, It just came over the radio: England has declared war on us, and they think France will do the same within hours!"

He took a long sip from his bottle. "Unless Hitler immediately withdraws his troops. I tell you, there is the second World War! He just went too far with his bluffing and gambling. God have mercy on all of us!"

He hurried down the steps and almost raced towards the gym. Suddenly he heaved his beer bottle against the brick wall, and it exploded into a thousand pieces.

"Verflucht! Verfluchte Scheisse!" I heard him cursing. "He is such a fool! And we Germans are fools! Oh, verdammte Scheisse!"

Another World War. I knew it was true. We all were stuck in it, there was no escape. We also knew that our youth was gone, forever.

Heinrich von Ellsleben, though, was triumphant. He started to strut across the large lawn. We could hear him sing verses of the infamous song about "...und heute gehoert uns Deutschland, and morgen die ganze Welt" ("Today Germany is ours, and tomorrow the whole world will be.") When he passed us on the way back he shot a contemptuous look at us, who were worried about the war more than anything else.

. . .

That night I had a strange dream. I was sitting around the campfire with those guys in Brazil, at the bank of a river, trying tequila and singing with them the song about the "Golden River". I just loved this song, but this time the men were different: they looked at me in a strange way, as if they were trying to pierce me with their stares.

The oldest man seemed to be friendlier. He said, "It is a long way to this river. You have to climb over high mountains. There is snow, and there are wild animals. But you are young. We never will make it in our age, we just think of doing it. Stick it out, boy, stick it out, and you will find that river."

The other guys laughed, apparently doubting my resolve. But I knew I was going to go for it. I will do it. I will do it.

I woke up, perspiring and exhausted, not really knowing where I was. Then I saw the half-vcamouflaged street lantern outside of my window and relaxed. I smiled at the fading vision of my dream.

. . .

CHAPTER 11

Signe called and asked me to go with her to a party at Wessel's. "I want to go with you, Dietz, Wolf has been not very nice lately."

Helga Wessel was a friend of hers. Once a year she gave a big party for her teenage friends.

The Wessels lived in a large house overlooking the Elbe River. From the patio you had a beautiful, almost endless view of the river. The parents had established the nice custom of flying the flags of the nations of almost any ship that came up the river. Now was war, though, and the custom was discontinued. The large flagpole was empty.

This would probably be the last of the big parties. Too many restrictions had been placed on the economy. The Wessels must have some connections, though. There was enough food and some wine. The parents themselves had some of their friends over and were sitting at a table somewhere removed, not wanting to appear too much like chaperones.

The party was good and lively. Everybody tried to be cheerful and relaxed, tried not to think of the war, and it did work. A record player brought us the music we wanted. A number of friends had brought their own jazz records.

We danced on the patio. A nice warm breeze came up from the river. The lights had been turned out everywhere because of the danger of air raids. That made for a weird scene, as we were dancing to candle light only.

As Signe and I moved to some blues melody, we saw Wolf dancing close to us. He was with Juanita Bauer, the daughter of Helga's neighbor. Juanita really clung to him, almost fused to his body. She saw us and then put both her arms around Wolf's neck, pulled him down to her and kissed him. When she let go, she shot a triumphant look at Signe. Well, she had Wolf for the evening.

I do not believe that Wolf was aware of what was going on between the two girls. Signe just shook her head and said something like "Ahem-", nothing else. But I knew about what she was thinking. We finished the dance.

"Dietz, let us have another glass of wine. I want to show you something then."

She had again a beautiful smile on her face, but this time it was not only devilish, it also was inviting and promising. We went together upstairs to a guest room and sat down on the bed. The room was furnished with rustic Austrian furniture: a high bed, a table, a chair and a cabinet. Pictures of the Tyrol area were on the walls.

"Dietz, I told you some time ago that I was not ready. Well, maybe I am now. No, not to go all the way, but--Dietz, there are other ways--that are safe. I think you know what I mean." She chuckled.

I went to the door and locked it, then turned off the light. I went to the camouflage shade and let it roll up. After I had opened the window the warm evening air came inside, and there was a full moon making everything look silvery. We first kissed slowly, searchingly, then let ourselves down on the bed.

We did what I had dreamed about since I first had met her. No, we did not lose control. It was wonderful and exciting.

We disengaged and sat there for a while. The party apparently was going great. We could hear the gang singing the Lambeth Walk. I was sure nobody missed us.

"Dietz...I like the way you did all this. You were so - gentle."

We got up and straightened our clothes. Both of us laughed when we saw the other one straightening out their hair. Somehow this seemed to be so funny.

"Signe, I think we should go downstairs now. Let's finish our wine and go."

The music was the kind we loved, and we went back and danced to the St. Louis Blues.

I now felt fairly safe with Signe. Wolf was out, at least for a while.

And we had not broken the pact. We did some heavy necking, yes, but it was so spontaneous, and most of all we stopped and did not go all the way. That we felt was the basic point in our pact. The way Juanita had wrapped herself around Wolf, I was sure they would do their share of necking that night too.

Anyway, this was not the time to enter any permanent relationship, at least not in my opinion. Everything was completely unsettled and would be for a long time.

. . .

Wolf and Signe made up. There was no sense becoming dramatic or possessive at this time, when actually bombs could wipe you out, or something else could happen any day.

No, I was not happy with this at all. I realized that I had the tendency to be possessive after all. Come on, Dietz, how would you claim her for life. With what? We all are searching, aren't we?

Look around! Let the winds of the world blow around your face for a while! A war is going on!

We all knew now for sure that we would have to go into the armed services, one way or the other. The best way, it seemed, was to volunteer for the branch of service you wanted to serve in rather than having to go to the infantry. At least we felt we might have some control over our fate. And -- the good thing was that we would be given our graduation papers if we volunteered .

Kurt told me that he would volunteer for the navy and try to study medicine as an ensign--not a bad idea. Walter Suessenheim volunteered for a famous cavalry regiment in Hanover, and they accepted him very soon. Wolf Rohrbach talked about going into the navy too, then made up his mind and applied.

At this time I dreaded nothing more than the infantry, where you marched and marched, swallowed all the dust and did all the dirty work. I wanted something motorized. For a while I thought of going to a tank unit. But how could you get out of a burning tank? Still, I volunteered, and by some stroke of luck a unit of a Panzerkorps sent me an acceptance note for their motorized signal corps company.

We boys discussed all the pros and cons. Everybody said the war would be over in a year or so.

By the spring of 1940 Germany invaded Norway and Denmark. Grab Norway and Denmark, keep England from getting there first, that was the rationale. The German troops suffered heavy losses in the fighting around

Narvik, and the navy sustained an almost mortal blow when some of their newest ships like the cruiser "Bluecher" and several destroyers were sunk.

Twelve hundred sailors died in the cold water when the "Bluecher" went down. The irony was that the ship was destroyed by shore batteries built years ago in Germany and then sold to the Norwegians. As usual they worked perfectly well. It took just a few rounds to sink the ship.

In May 1940 suddenly the "real" war was on. The small countries like Belgium had been promised neutrality, but they were overrun by the German military machine. The fanfares sounded almost every hour on the radio announcing one victory after another. Reports came almost endlessly, stating that certain cities had been taken, or that so and so many prisoners and so and so many tanks or pieces of artillery were ours. Some people almost became hysterical: What an army! What a glorious German army! The war will be over soon!

But a strange thing happened. At the height of the campaign in France, Hitler stopped his Panzerkorps from taking the channel towns like Dunquerque, where hundreds of thousands of British soldiers were trapped, waiting to be evacuated to England. Why? Did Hitler want to save Britain some embarrassment? Did he want to save "Nordic" blood? Or did he expect that Britain would make peace if he saved these lives?

Something was definitely fishy. The Generals called on Hitler again and again and demanded that he should finish the campaign right there.

No. Hitler said no. The generals obeyed.

. . .

There was not too much I had been able to plan to do with Signe. First I was caught in the air raid duty, just like Wolf was. Neither of us had much time off. But the fact that he had dated her and probably called her on the phone placed a shadow on our relationship. I did not want to be jealous, but you know how it is.

After a few weeks our "job" as air raid warden was terminated, and school life seemed to return to about what it had been before.

Immediately after the war had started food was greatly restricted. You had to have coupons for everything from butter to sugar. The grocery stores were soon empty, and not even soda or pop was available. Wine and anything special became extremely hard to get.

This stopped all parties for practical purposes. Even the restaurants had nothing to offer except on coupons. It was like in jail, all initiative was killed. It made no sense taking a job on the side because you could not buy anything. I could not get any gas for the motorcycle, and nobody was there to do repair work on it. Most mechanics had been drafted to the armed forces, and those who remained home had more important things to do than to repair a motorcycle for a young guy. Let him use his bicycle...

There was one problem that was very hard to answer. Why were people so willing to accept all these restrictions, why did they now pride themselves saying that they could manage somehow, just give them a chance to try? Was that dumb pride in their adaptability, their chance to invent solutions?s? "Yes, we have done all this during the last war too. Remember how we had no food? How we practically lived on turnips and potatoes?"

Why would they accept all trouble so easily? Instead of being more realistic, and look around and see that this all was an impossible task? Instead of counting how many nations we had against us? Instead of looking at all the injustice which was being done already at that time. Why did they not object to Germany breaking Holland and Belgium's neutrality? I did not have answers for all these questions.

Signe, Wolf and I were now more like a threesome, spending our time together, usually at Wolf's house in front of the radio.

Wolf received his notice to report to a navy base camp in Bremerhaven. Wolf, Signe and I met for the last time in his house.

Signe was late, so we talked and listened to records. We felt uncomfortable and ill at ease. We did not want to be dramatic, but after all a war was going on. Everything felt a little meaningless and hollow as we were talking until I remembered that I wanted to discuss something special with Wolf.

"Wolf, have you ever thought of what might happen if we get captured and become prisoners-of-war? Do we have any legal protection, or can they do with us what they want to do? Isn't there something like a Geneva Convention, or is it the Haag Conference--dealing with these problems?"

"Dietz, I think it is the Geneva Convention," he answered, "about avoiding cruelties against the enemy. I know the British and French will honor it, but the Poles--I am not absolutely sure whether I myself would be perfectly fair to soldiers who have attacked by a country."

"I know what you mean. Let's look up what is written in their summary."

"Yes, we should do that," Wolf said.

"Are there any guide lines for us, for ourselves, so we don't have to--you know what I mean--injure or kill prisoners, use unnecessary roughness or things like that, I mean, if they command us to do that?"

"I don't know." Wolf looked pensive. "We...just have to make up our mind not to do those things...."

I interrupted him. "There is a good word for this: Decency, stay decent, use decency, be a gentleman whenever you can!"

"Yes, that sounds pretty good. That sounds realistic, we can work with that. It is a practical religious command. Decency...I can accept that."

At this time the door bell rang. It was Signe.

"Sorry I am late. I had an errand to make which took longer than I thought. What are you guys talking about? You look so serious. Anything important?"

"Hi, Signe", I said. I noticed a slight pang of jealousy. Cut it out, Dietz, I thought. This is no time to claim possession.

I continued. "We were talking about what protection we will have as prisoners,and how we can protect ourselves against having to commit cruelties against prisoners of our own."

"We think that there are some rules laid down in the Geneva Convention, and we want to check on that," Wolf added.

"You are serious, you two, aren't you? But I think it is wonderful that you are doing this. Let us make a pact, a promise not to act cruelly in this war. Yes, I know, I am not in it, but I love both of you, and I want to be your...witness."

This girl had a wonderful attitude. Wolf and I looked at each other. We both must have simultaneously stood up and we all put our right hands on top of each other. It was so spontaneous that we all smiled.

"Okay, be it this way," Signe said. We all sat down. Wolf turned the radio up. We could get New York, but the reception was not that good. It was much more warbled than in the early morning.

Signe reported some rumors she had heard on a Swedish radio station saying that Hitler had decided not to invade England this year. He was not well enough prepared and did not have enough ships and barges. The

British had reported that Germany lost too many planes when bombing London and other cities.

Signe surprised us: "I told you that I love both of you. But there is not time to go any farther right now. Let's keep our friendship as it is until we can see clear, until the war is over."

What a girl. Wolf and I looked at each other, and both of us nodded.

It must have been about four weeks since he enlisted when Wolf got his first leave. He came to visit the class and naturally was the center of attention. He seemed to enjoy it, but to me he seemed depressed. His spark and enthusiasm wasn't there, he did not look well and seemed to have gained weight. Gaining weight in basic training?

Finally we got together for a short time. I asked how everything had been, whether basic training really was so rough.

"No, Dietz, I took it pretty well. Actually, I gained a few pounds."

After a short period of hesitation he continued, somewhat haltingly. "You know, Dietz, it is different. Once your superiors know that you are an officer's candidate and will go on to better things, they want to show how powerful they are. I mean the corporals and sergeants.

Also, everybody there knows by now that I was born and raised in Singapore. They love to make me aware that I am in the German navy now, not somewhere else. Most of them have been made to believe that we can conquer England in no time, particularly with our strong air force preparing their country. I know that it is not going to be that easy no matter what they say.

"I don't want to complain too much. As I look around, though, everybody tells me that all officer's positions are filled, and that the only way to faster advancement is to volunteer for the submarines. The chances are good there."

"Submarines? You are crazy! I am sorry, but they are death traps!" I really got upset.

"It's all right, Dietz", he said. "Nowadays they have much better safety features, like better escape hatches and stronger hulls to withstand depth charges. The construction is different now, they say. Also," he grinned somewhat awkwardly, "there is no safer place in an Atlantic storm than at the bottom of the sea."

"Depth charges, what about them? No matter what, that is the greatest danger!"

"Well,...I will go for it anyhow. You know that I am not a career man. I just want to get my Lieutenant or First Lieutenant. By then the war will be over and I can get out of the navy."

I still was upset. Submarines would be the last service I would volunteer for.

We celebrated later on with Signe. Wolf's father had found a good bottle of wine. We all felt as if the sword of Damocles was hanging over our heads. The war would last only a short time, wouldn't it? We were not so sure anymore.

. . .

Wolf was gone now, and I did not expect to wait much longer for my appointment to go to the service.

I did not feel at ease to date Signe now. One reason was that I did not want to take advantage of her since she had made it clear that she was not going any further with either one of us until we knew more about our future, that is how long this stupid war would take. The other reason was that everybody felt generally worried about the war, about soldiers now dying. It was not a joyful time.

I had to see Signe, though, one more time. I wanted to take some pictures of her and of both of us. I called her up and we met in her yard. No, you could not visit a girl inside her house. That was impossible.

I got my camera ready, and I took some pictures of her, close ups of her face, of her standing and leaning on a tree. Then she took a few of me in similar situations.

Suddenly she had a very sheepish look on her face.

"Dietz," she said, "wait for a minute. I have something upstairs. I will be right back."

She ran inside and came back in a minute or two, still with that devilish look on her face. "Dietz--I had these pictures taken in Stockholm. My sister lives there. She is married and has a photo studio, and she is quite good. She wanted me to pose..."

She showed a few very good pictures, actually portraits, and then a few seminude and completely nude photos of herself.

I dropped my jaw. Brother!

"Take them, please. They are not so prude up there in Sweden, and a lot of us girls have similar pictures. We are adults, aren't we? I will send some to Wolf too."

Yes, I put the pictures into my wallet while my brain was tumbling. It took me a minute to regain my composure. "Signe, thanks, thanks very much. I will keep them, that's for sure, I will keep them close to me.

Yes, I want to say good-bye now, in case we will not meet before I leave. It is great to have these pictures...all of them.

I will write to you. I want to stay in touch with you. Good luck! I love you!"

"Dietz, I will write too. I love you too."

Man, that was great, that is her maturity and her trust. With her trust she had given me more than if I had slept with her, and I did not have to worry about her getting pregnant.

I was upset when my mother told me that my brother Pat had been drafted for the Work Service Corps. These men had to do heavy physical work, building roads or working on barracks, building fortifications in the West. That was crazy! How could they make him do that? He would get his attacks that way; there was no doubt about it.

After a few weeks Pat had an attack of paralysis. He was miserable. He finally was sent to a hospital and then discharged from the service. His professor in Freiburg was very helpful and arranged for him to resume his studies. And I now worried more and more whether I would get this disease too. They said you would not get it once you were over sixteen years old.

After a few weeks a little card came in the mail notifying me that I should report to the signal corps unit in Weimar, Thuringia, on the fourth of December, 1940.

So, that was it then.

Actually my departure was very unemotional. My mother had not tried to talk me out of going. She probably realized that I would have to go one of these days anyhow, and I had explained to her the reason why I wanted to stay ahead of the game.

Maybe she was also glad that I was going away. We had been silently fighting all these months, mainly because of her relationship with Vinci. She must have noticed that I had lost all respect for her.

Of all things Vinci came too when I was about to leave. Vinci, who was such a pathetic guy. He tried to be important, talked about his experience

71

in the First World War as an infantry man. He had been one of those "elders", who always emphasized the educational value of having withstood a severe barrage of artillery fire, which they had named "Trommelfeuer". Without this experience you just did not count in this life, he said. I did not pay any attention to him. I had heard that story so many times.

Then I stood in the corridor of the express train and watched as the city and suburbs of Hamburg fell away and then pastures, later on barren fields and little villages passed by.

The saying was that the army was not yet politically tainted and overall did not care about the Nazis. They still felt that they were the highly estimated German institution with a long tradition of victories. Maybe I could get a break somewhere and collect enough points so that later on I could go on without the help of the Nazis.

Suddenly a whole stream of doubts entered my mind. Why was I doing this? Why did I not stay home? Why had I enlisted? Was it only because I could choose where I wanted to go? Or was I afraid I would not be able to pass the graduation examination and by failing it would ruin my mother's reputation as a tutor? If you volunteered you got that examination automatically. . .Yes, some of this was true.

Or was it that I was so ashamed of my mother because of her affair with a married man, claiming that this all was for" educational purposes", even when they went off for "hiking trips" for the whole weekend and left me alone - - - What would my friends think about that if they knew? My future was already threatened by the fact that she had been divorced, and now she made it worse by running around with a married man.

No, I had to leave. And the army was my only chance. I hated war, hated to think that I would have to kill. I also hated the thought that my friends now would believe I was an ardent Nazi, running like this to the army.

I had to leave, find out what life and war was about. The war would be over soon, they said, and I hoped that I would have found a more positive solution by then.

I now had left the awful, dead home, where there were constant complaints about not having any money, the fights between my grandmother and my mother, the lack of fun and hope, and being without a father. I would now be out of the control zone of my mother, and away from Vinci.

Army life would not be easy, and, no question, you could get killed. But I did not think of that too much. I would be on my own. Hopefully

I would not destroy my chances to return one day and study something. All the teachers had said it would be difficult to resume studying after a long absence. Well, I would have to see.

The train gathered speed, the wheels clattering over switches and howling in the curves.

I was not sentimental about Signe. The thought of her was wonderful, she would be in my mind all the time. How could I ask for anything else?

I was surprised that I already felt some spirit of adventure, a little taste of freedom. No more school, no more useless Greek lessons, no more endless marching and singing in the Hitler Youth.

Long stretches of heather and forests passed by. Click-click-clack, click-click-clack--that was the sound of the train wheels, almost putting me to sleep. Sleep? No way, Dietz! You will have to be alert and sharp, everyday, every minute of this adventure! Maybe for a year or so. By then I had done my duty, and the war would be over.

. . .

CHAPTER 12

The train arrived in Weimar in the early afternoon. I checked in with my unit, the training company of the Weimar battalion of the signal corps. Some of the new arrivals had been assigned to the telephone units. They had to carry heavy cables across the terrain and establish phone connection, frequently under heavy enemy fire. I was lucky. I was assigned to the wireless section, the radio operators.

All army barracks in the city already were overcrowded. We were housed in an old abandoned school building that apparently had not been ventilated for years and the air was suffocating.

The usual basic training started. It was by far not as tough as I had anticipated. The years of pre-military training in the Hitler Youth had prepared us well. We laughed at the chicanery some of the sergeants tried on us. Overall they could not impress us with their tricks.

"There's one thing you have to learn, Dietz" one of the older fellows said. "Whenever you cross the courtyard or go anywhere, put on an expression of extreme seriousness and involvement, and always walk fast. The non-coms will think you have a job to do and won't bother you."

Radioman first class Erwin Muschel was my immediate superior. He loved to rib the newly-arrived high school boys, most of them had been assigned to the wireless section, and he believed it was his job to introduce us to the realities of life.

"Heller," he said. "You all have heard so much about the great poets and writers Goethe and Schiller, both of whom lived here in Weimar at one time or the other,- - but did you know that Goethe wrote on his last day of life that he had intercourse with a young woman the night before?" Then he added "Heller, did you know that Goethe and Schiller at one time

75

were involved with each other on a homosexual basis?" He quoted a little ditty that described the way those two supposedly made love. I did not even know men did it that way. So what. Goethe and Schiller? I had given up on them since a long time.

Muschel had been a teacher and was quite intelligent, but he also was sharp-tongued. He moved around like Napoleon Bonaparte, short, stocky, his chest sticking out forward all the time. He seemed to be so self-important. But he was a good instructor, teaching Morse code, coding and decoding and the basic electronics of wireless radio.

These were important subjects, I thought. Let him think that he is Napoleon. I'd better learn all this well, or they will send me to the telephone troops.

He must have taken a liking to me, as I had to him. One day he came over as I was scrubbing the floor.

"Heller,...I want to take you to the Dive-Bomber Bar. I want to show you a part of life you have never even dreamed about!"

I did not know what to say, I was shocked he would ask a recruit, breaching the great barrier which existed even between the lowest non-com and a new soldier. We had heard about this place. It was supposed to be really raunchy and loud and wild. Some guys had said it was a brothel.

"Be ready at seven-thirty tonight" Muschel said insinuatingly. "Fritz Runge will come too."

This sounded like a pretty good adventure; let's try it.

The bar was located in West Weimar. We had to take a bus and then walk half a mile. There were no taxis around.

We could hear singing even before we entered. The place was filled with smoke and you sure could smell that this was a beer place. It was packed with air force men and some army soldiers. In one corner there was a group of giggling air force helper girls in their blue uniforms, surrounded from all sides by the soldiers. There were no officers to be seen.

At the far end of the large room was a stage with a small pit in front. Four elderly civilian musicians tried to penetrate the noise playing loudly and poorly. Everybody seemed to be in a very good mood. I caught some fragments of conversation where pilots vividly described their bombing runs, smashing bridges or gasoline storage tanks.

Muschel led us to a table, stopping to say hello to this one and that one, and quite a few men waved back to him. We ordered some beer.

One of Muschel's friends came over. He was a tall corporal with an Iron Cross first class on his uniform jacket.

"Muschel, do you know the latest about Ilse Koch?"

"No, what has she done now?" Ilse Koch was the wife of the commandant of a concentration camp near Weimar and she was known for her cruelty.

"She is taking skin from prisoners who have died,...wherever she can find a good tattoo, she had it prepared and has lampshades made of it: you know, pictures of breasts and tits and so on."

"What? That is crazy! I don't believe it!" Muschel was getting upset.

"Believe me, it is true. I know it from a friend of mine who is an SS guard up there. He knows...." The corporal left, satisfied that he had made a deep impression on us.

At that time Fritz Runge got up, grabbed his mouth and ran out of the room. I wish I could have reacted the same way, but I could not for some reason. I just felt dizzy.

I have to give credit to Muschel. He looked pale. He got up and said "Heller, let's go. That's not what I wanted to show you."

Earlier I had figured out what he really wanted me to see. Soldiers had started to shout, "Where are the girls? Bring the girls on!"

Muschel and I left, leaving some money on the table. We found Fritz outside of the building. He still did some retching, but otherwise he was all right.

No one spoke on the way back to our quarters. Each one of us tried to find a way to handle the story of the cadaver skin.

None of the people I met in our unit would have been as depraved as this woman, the wife of an SS officer, turned out to be. Maybe the army was naive, but they still were civilized, they were mainly civilians in uniform, or if they felt stronger about everything, they were proud members of this Prussian type of army. There was no direct Nazi propaganda.

I had guessed right, and I felt lucky.

. . .

"Richie, Richie Gattorna!" I could not believe it. "You are going to be with us?"

There stood my friend. I had no idea that he was coming here to Weimar. What a stroke of luck to have a good friend here. He was put into another troup, though, but we could get together easily.

I helped him with his luggage and we talked a while about Hamburg and the school and our friends. Most of them had volunteered like we did and were waiting to be called up.

"A good day for me." I said to myself.

. . .

Basic training was not going to last forever. After about eight weeks we learned that we would be assigned to some active unit, may in Poland or France, or in the newly established Africa Corps.

One bitter-cold day in February a solid blanket of snow covered the area. We were going out again in a radio truck to establish radio contact with the home basis. Usually we parked the truck near a farmhouse, and one guy went over to the house to try to buy some butter or sausage, whatever was available, while the other ones worked on the assignment. Muschel always approved of those buying trips as long as we did not forget him.

We were a few miles north of Weimar and we passed an endless high fence on the left side of the road. The truck crept slowly up the hill struggling on the icy road. Then we passed a big gate, and there were some SS men standing guard.

"What is this?" I asked.

"Buchenwald," Muschel said. "You know what that is, don't you? It is a large concentration camp," he continued without waiting for an answer. He now had a strained look on his face. "It's for communists, political out-laws, former union leaders and homosexuals. Be glad you are not in there."

I felt for a moment as if a blast of very cold and deadly air had passed by, much colder than it was on the outside. Some of us looked at each other with a questioning expression. Nobody, though, said anything.

The truck kept on climbing the long hill. Concentration camps? This subject was taboo. No discussion was allowed in public. Ever since the fire at the "Reichstag" in 1934 the Nazis imprisoned political enemies, to be held until after the victory. Nobody ever heard stories of prisoners who had left those camps.

. . .

The next morning the master sergeant called for me and gave me my assignment. Richie Gattorna, my friend from Hamburg, and I were going to join a unit in southwest France near Bordeaux.

What a lucky break! Out of this cold winter into sunny France? I had heard that soldiers had gone swimming there, even right after Christmas. Palm trees, subtropical climate--great.

Had Muschel helped a little to get this assignment? I did not know. Maybe. Or was it the old, one-armed sergeant, who in his grumbling voice had said, "Heller, Gattorna, you two blokes from Hamburg, you might as well stay together."

In my excitement I thought it might be a good idea to say good-bye to Muschel and some of the other instructors. Well, I came to regret that decision very soon.

I had walked over to the sergeant's quarters, where I knew Muschel was staying. I knocked at the door.

"Come in!" somebody inside barked.

I entered and saluted. "I want to say good-bye. I will be transferred to a unit in France. Thanks for--"

"Are you completely crazy, soldier?" One of the sergeants shot up, while everybody in the room stopped talking. "Soldier, you are in the German army, not on a family picnic or on a school outing! 'Radioman Heller is asking permission to report his transfer to an active unit in whatever it is, wherever it may be.' That's the way you should say it!"

He turned to his buddies, roaring with laughter. "He says he wants to say "Good-bye"! Maybe he brought some flowers too!" He could not stop laughing. The other sergeants laughed too, and Muschel gave me a look that indicated I was definitely a hopeless case.

I felt my face flush. I saluted fast and backed out of the room as quickly as I could, feeling flustered and angry. Really, I should have known better. How could I expect those hard-boiled sergeants to respond any differently. I felt like a fool.

In a flash vision I also saw there would be a danger for me in the army, run-ins with sergeants and officers of this type, who delighted in jumping on anybody who displayed an unmilitary attitude.

I will not turn into one of those human machines without feeling, I resolved. The war cannot last that long, and then I will be a civilian again.

· · ·

CHAPTER 13

Weimar to Paris to Bordeaux. It sounded so great. The trip brought Richie Gattorna and me from the cold winter in Thuringia first to Paris, and it was already considerably warmer there. We had no time to sightsee and had to go on immediately to the Gare d'Orleans to get the express train to Bordeaux.

One historic town after another passed: Orleans, Tours, Poitier and later on the little town of Cognac, where the name of the brandy came from. Finally we were approaching Bordeaux. I opened the window and could smell spring air.

`I was standing in the corridor of the train, letting the landscape pass by. Somehow I felt uncomfortable traveling through France. "What are you doing here, Dietz? Didn't you want to save a trip to France for peaceful days, and not as a soldier? Who is paying your fare? It is the German army, isn't it? You don't think that suddenly everything is right because you were given a good assignment?"

A little voice inside of me had suddenly spoken. No, I knew it wasn't right.

"Dietz," the voice went on, "you'd better remember that your great-grandmother's parents came from France. They had moved to Guadaloupe and then were driven off that island by an uprising of the natives and settled in New Orleans--but still, they were French. These are your own people, here, right before your eyes!"

A second voice came up, sounding more like my own.

"Okay, there is a war going on. I did not start it, and I am against it. Now I will have to deal with all this. Give me a break. I will find out where I really belong--but give me some time!"

I knew very well that both voices had a point, and I knew they would be coming back again and again, especially the voice that challenged me for being in France. This would make it hard to enjoy my time here, but I knew the voice was right.

Bordeaux was overflowing with German soldiers, officers and army vehicles. We even saw a few tanks near the commandantura.

I wish I could believe wholeheartedly in this great display of German military might - all these sharp-looking officers and men with their Iron Crosses and other decorations gleaming in the sunlight. Everyone seemed to be very proud and happy. The soldiers standing guard at the commandantura presented their rifles to any officer or non-com, endlessly, tirelessly, beaming with scarcely hidden pride. I almost could believe that there was no army in this world that could measure up to those troops.

I felt proud too, but the voices had started to nag me and had made me aware that there were forces stronger than the armed forces: that my conscience had been alerted, and that I could not deny that I had a strong guilt feeling.

What was the name of my French forefathers? It was LeJendre. As if I did not know.

We boarded a local train to go further southwest. Our final stop was a resort town called Arcachon. When we climbed out of the train we immediately smelled the salty and rich air coming from the Bay of Biscay. What a delightful air it was!

Richie and I both were almost intoxicated by this air, the warmth of it and the variety of strange and exciting aromas. We looked at each other, smiling. We felt we were in dreamland.

For the first time in our lives we saw palm trees lining the boulevard and strange and exotic plants and flowers along the road. Ahead of us, towards the Basin d'Arcachon, was a big casino.

A soldier in the black uniform of the tank troops came up, waving to us. "Are you the two new guys from Weimar? Glad I got you in time. They did not let me go until now."

He noticed that we were looking around, scanning the area. He was eager to explain our new location.

"Yes, this city is situated on a bay, the Basin d'Arcachon. Lots of oyster fishing here...boating, swimming. On the other side of the bay is a long peninsula, with a village called Cap Ferret, and from there on it is all ocean for thousands of miles. You know, the Biscaya. You have read about it?"

We strolled down a wide promenade towards the bay. I studied the soldier. He was wearing what would be our new uniform: black fall trousers, a black short jacket, and yellow insignia at the collar indicating that we belong to the communication troops. There was a skull and crossbones insignia on the collar too. How did they get that? I wondered. Skull and crossbones usually were reserved for SS units. They better have nothing to do with the SS! I wanted army, not SS.

Fortunately I remembered that the "Hussars"--cavalry troops--had taken on the duty of scouting in older armies. Much of that activity had been taken over by fully motorized communication troops. Their emblem remained to be the skull and crossbones. I felt relieved.

We came to a restaurant and hotel on the corner of a large boulevard. The soldier motioned us to enter. He seemed to enjoy our hesitation and astonishment.

"Yes, we are living in this hotel, the 'Hotel Moderne'. It is great fun, you will like it. I will show you your rooms. Heller, you are going to stay with Pfc. Georg Osten, and you, Gattorna-is that your name?-will go with me to the other end of the hotel."

At the top of the stairs was my room. "This is Pfc. Osten's room," the guide said. "There is one bed--you have to sleep with him. It's still better than being in barracks. Osten is your immediate superior. You have to follow his orders. Good luck!"

Sleep with another guy in the same bed? I felt really embarrassed. You know, all those stories I had heard...

I looked around. I saw an array of perfume bottles, jars with cream and hair lotions on the dresser.

Dietz, be positive, I said to myself. It does not have to mean anything. Wait until you meet this guy, then you can judge.

I started to unpack, taking care not to disturb Osten's room arrangement. Suddenly the door opened.

"Hi, Heller--that is your name, isn't it? I am Georg Osten. Welcome to France!"

He was perfectly natural and not effeminate at all. Georg was fairly short and moved around a little bit like a jungle cat would move--like Wolf Rohrbach. His features were somewhat Asiatic, but he had large and sensitive eyes. His voice was deep and throaty. I noticed that the second and third finger of his right hand were yellowish stained, probably from smoking a lot.

No, he was not a problem. We got along well immediately. He took me down to the restaurant and we tried to get some eggs and toast. My first attempt to speak French turned out to be a complete disaster. I became confused and Osten had to help. We laughed.

The next day I received my new black uniform that fitted well, and I thought I looked sharp. Everything was exciting so far. I saw Richie a few times and he said he felt the same way--giddy, excited, wasn't-it-great-to-be-here, full of anticipation.

It did not last long. Reality, cruel and harsh, hit the next day. On morning roll call a sergeant reported that the field gendarmery had executed two French partisans. The day before they had interrupted the army phone cable between Paux and Biarritz and had stolen the copper wires.

". . . you would have done something like that if your country had been invaded, Dietz." The little voice was here again.

"I believe I would have. Maybe not stealing copper wire, but maybe something else."

Yes, I would have. I knew I would have at least tried.

Nobody else seemed to be upset about this killing: at least I did not see anybody, who was. . .

CHAPTER 14

While Georg Osten and I got along very well, I still found it strange to sleep with a man in the same bed. I pretended that there was nothing unusual about it, which eliminated potential embarrassing discussions. I took care not to touch Georg inadvertently during my sleep.

Well, nothing ever happened. Georg usually came in very late at night, whistling some hit tune. Most of the time he had a noticeable smell of alcohol on him. He did not say much and fell right asleep.

As I found out later, Georg was having a heyday with the French girls. He entertained them with tales like, "I am so lonely here," or "I might have to go to battle tomorrow, and who knows? I might get killed."

Some of the girls fell for this line. One night during the ultimate intimacy his girlfriend had a spasm and they could not separate--like dogs. Somebody called an ambulance, which brought both of them to a hospital in Bordeaux. The doctors there took care of the situation.

Naturally there was always somebody who delighted in telling this story. As much as he hated it, Georg had to smile with them. This story had become known to the company commander, and it took Georg longer to make corporal than anybody else.

It took me a while to understand Sergeant Heinrich Bass, my troup leader. He was one of the many tall men I was meeting: everybody was tall except Kretschmar, Schmitt and Georg Osten. Bass also unfortunately was very ugly and his face had a dour expression. Sure, that was not his fault, and I felt somewhat sorry for him. Maybe that's what made him at times so awfully moody.

What bothered me was that he was so methodical in every thing he did or said. He picked on me and made a big issue out of every little irregularity I might have committed.

One day he called me to his room. "Radioman Heller, I have been observing you. I have the feeling that there are many things you don't agree with. I want you to know that the army goes by the Army Service Instruction Manual, yes, word for word, letter by letter. Once you are a general you can start thinking of changing it, not before. Right now it will be better for you to act according to it. Dismissed!"

How did he know that I felt exactly like that--that I wanted to have the privilege to change things or at least discuss them? How could he tell that being in the army for me was a necessary evil, while he himself loved to be in it?

However, I realized that Bass basically was a very fair person, and that he excelled in management of his radio routines. I wanted to learn them as well as I could. Otherwise he would have me completely in his hands.

. . .

One evening I was sitting in the movie room at the casino. I noticed a good-looking infantry soldier in front of me. A beautiful French girl was with him. She was gazing at him adoringly. During intermission the soldier was talking to her, apparently translating a German love song that had appeared again and again in the movie. It was a very slow and sensuous song, in which the girl singer sang again and again, "I want to be to you what you want me to be. Do with me what you want. I want to be your slave of love."

Are you naive? I wondered. The French girl has a right to do what she wants. If she loves this German soldier, let it be. You are just jealous. Are you missing someone, maybe? Well, I knew the answer to that. I knew I had her very much in my mind, maybe temporarily pushed in the background. Who could blame me?

Still, I was disappointed that this girl would swoon so much over a soldier of the occupying forces, and I hated that anybody wanted to be a "slave of love." I hated anybody who would want to call himself a slave.

But then it was different the next day. We were driving to the park a few miles along the basin, where we kept all our trucks and cars. We passed a group of French girls, who kept their heads high, looking neither right or left and did not respond to the whistling and calling of the German soldiers. I felt happy, even proud of them.

In a few days I found myself totally involved in daily routines, working with the radio equipment, transmitting, receiving, getting faster and more experienced. Osten and my sergeant also made me clean the rooms, since I was the newcomer.

Then one afternoon Georg Osten grabbed my sleeve and had me follow him to the room where the receivers were lined up. "Hurry up, Dietz! We want to listen to the 'Boss'. He is on at 5 p.m. Hurry!"

In the room were a few other soldiers. They all looked overly casual, as if they had something to hide.

"What is this all about, Georg?"

Georg always like to be a little dramatic, and he held his index finger to his lips. "Just listen, Dietz!"

Suddenly the other soldiers went to other receivers and turned on the sets, and so did Georg.

We could hear Morse code. It was the letter "V": did-did-did-da, repeated over and over.

"Dietz, this is a secret British radio station. A lot of us guys listen to it. Their call sign is the "V", like the British have elected "V" for victory. Now listen!"

The did-did-did-da stopped. A man they called the "Boss" started to speak. He had a deep voice, tough and authoritative. He gave war news in German and then asked whatever happened to the German people, the people of poets, of musicians and thinkers. Why did they have to start another war? Hadn't Germany and Austria started the last Great War? Didn't they know that again the whole world would get together and fight back?

The other soldiers laughed, feeling apparently supremely self-assured and showing distaste for this poor radio announcer. I watched Georg. He did not seem to be sure of all this. Neither was I. The "Boss" continued.

"What about your invasion? What happened? Could it be that you are no match for the British Navy? Or that your air forces just could not break the will of our air force? Last year you lost over eight hundred planes and their crews. Well, if you try it again,   this summer, we will be ready for you."

He then switched to an imaginary scene at the English coast, painting a picture of the German Navy trying to land on the beaches. Their ships were being destroyed by the British Navy or the coast batteries. Now gasoline and oil had been set afire, burning all over the area. It was described as an inferno. He pretended to be a German soldier. "Help, help, our boat is sunk. There is fire all over on the water! Peter and Kurt are already afire, they are screaming. Help! Now the flames are coming over here. I am burning now too...help!"

Naturally, all this was fake, but it was impressive. Georg remained silent. He then turned our set off. Some of the other soldiers did the same.

Georg cleared his throat. "Dietz, usually he is much funnier, not that drastic. Forget about it."

This was pretty strong propaganda, though. It had started to sink in, though. Hitler had to cancel his invasion last fall. The losses of the air force had been too great. He did not have enough ships and barges, and his navy was not strong enough to protect his troops.

What was more confusing and irritating was that Hitler did not seem to have made up his mind to destroy England--no matter what he said in his speeches.

What would Hitler do now? Would he behave like a rejected lover, maybe almost insane from his defeat, and turn to his second choice. Who was it going to be? Gibraltar? The Balkan States?

. . .

I had heard much talk about our company leader, Lieutenant Hornberg. Nobody had anything good to say about him. I finally met him and I immediately realized what the guys had been talking about. He was the slickest, best-uniformed officer I had ever seen. He had his uniform tailor-made in Hamburg, probably at enormous cost. But the weirdest thing was his monocle in his right eye, which made him look like a Prussian general staff officer, vintage 1914. The piercing, blue eyes made the effect even worse. Georg Osten was particularly angry about his "Super-Prussian" behavior. By now I knew that Georg Osten was a pretty sensitive guy, and despite his great weakness for women, or maybe because of it, he had definite feelings about what was humane behavior and what was not. I liked Georg for that.

He theorized at times that the new German officer should be more like a comrade than like a superior, not like the class-conscious officers of the Imperial Germany. Lieutenant Hornberg had not managed to step down from his pedestal. He even refused to wear the new and practical black uniform of the tank troops. No, he seemed to be too dignified to wear it. Somehow successfully he insisted on wearing his field-gray outfit. Did he not want to realize that he was now in Hitler's Nazi Army, not in a German-Prussian traditional unit?

Why did I instinctively fear this man?

We met for the first time on a narrow spiral staircase in the hotel. I stepped back a little bit to let the lieutenant pass, so I did not have enough space to raise my arm in the normal way to salute him without hitting his face.

"Bad salute, soldier!" Hornberg screamed with a surprisingly whiny voice, and kept on climbing the staircase. From the way he said it, I knew that this officer had filed me in his memory as a completely deficient and worthless soldier.

After a few days I met Karl Weber. He had been on assignment in Bordeaux. He told me that he was from Berlin, had graduated from high school and wanted to be an accountant after the war. He seemed to be very intelligent, smart and adaptable to almost any situation with a keen sense of self-preservation.

Our troup had one radio truck and one all-terrain vehicle. Franz Hesse was the driver for our truck most of the time. He was a young man from Leipzig. But he was hard to get to know, did not talk much. For some reason Heinz Kretschmar, who was the part-time driver of either vehicle, was very reserved too. Heinz missed his home life, he told me at one time. I had heard that both guys, Franz and Heinz, had some problems with their love life in this city which they abandoned with temptations.

Karl Schmitt was another member of the troup, about thirty-five years old, streetwise, but not unpleasant. At one time he had been in jail. He never told us any details, and we did not ask. Years earlier he had been in a car accident and lost a few front teeth. He never got dentures made. This made him look a little odd.

Karl loved the nightlife and the girls in this city. He spent his allowance in houses of ill repute and--took photographs, all of ladies of the night, naked, in all positions. He said that these pictures were his treasure. "One day we might be in a lonely spot, with girls far away, and we have to have something to strengthen our mind!"

He did not want to show the pictures to me, but Georg Osten said, "Hey, Karl, show them to Dietz. It won't be long before he has his own experiences here."

I smiled and did not any anything. I had better pictures than he did.

. . .

CHAPTER 15

We were going to get a new machine that would code and decode all messages very fast, changing clear text to code text and vice versa. Word had it that it was vastly superior to the old system, where we had to hand-code and decode the messages. All our radio traffic was in telegraphy; we never used voice communication.

Within a few days some of these machines arrived. It was the famous "Enigma" machine. It looked like a kind of typewriter and was very heavy. On opening you could see three rotors with many adjustable positions, and the front section contained many little cables and plugs for further adjustment. It had keys like a typewriter, which you had to press hard, and they moved slowly.

Hornberg demonstrated it with great pride. "This machine is absolutely safe. The enemy never will be able to decode our messages. You will have to sacrifice your life before you let one of these machines get into the enemy's hands, you understand?"

"Yes, sir," we all answered in unison.

We eagerly learned to use this machine. It saved so much time. You could type your message on the keys, and the scrambled text immediately appeared as the letters lit up on the panel. The second man read off the letters to a third man, who would write them down and give it to the radio operator to be sent immediately. Decoding was fast too. Frequently the message was decoded almost as the last group of words arrived, and it could be sent immediately to the superior.

We all thought it was a great invention and nobody ever would be able to break our code.

. . .

Soldiers were everywhere in the city of Arcachon, filling every hotel and every private pension. It was quite a spectacle to see the rough soldiers doing some of their weapon drills on the porches of resort hotels with their boot nails screeching on the marble tiles.

In the afternoon soldiers combed the city for something they could send home as a present.

At night we frequently had to stand guard in the park where we kept all of our vehicles. The park was a few miles out of town, on a large estate with a mansion on a little hill. It overlooked a wooded area extending down to the bay. The guardhouse was a lovely little pavilion right at the water's edge, with red-carpeted walls--an ideal place for lovers to meet.

For a moment I wondered whether I should sit down there and look at Signe's pictures--hell, I was not that much deprived yet. I loved making my rounds at night with a silvery moon reflected in the dark waters of the bay. I listened to the endless murmurs of the waves. A warm wind from the west frequently blew in from the Biscay and made the pine trees rustle.

After a few weeks I found that army life was tolerable. The unit had settled into a fairly easy routine. Nobody made a great fuss about politics, and the Nazis did not run it at all. I clearly noticed this and enjoyed the change. Sure, I was in the claws of the army, but it was pleasantly different. The perennial talk about heroic deeds and suffering of the World War I generation was replaced by the stories of accomplishments of the present army, and there was no question that they were justified. Fortunately the guys did not make you feel overly inferior.

The commander, Captain Schultz, was a slightly phlegmatic person from Hessia. In private life he was a lawyer. He liked his wine, and he had no ambition to become a hero.

I was very fortunate to be in this unit. I tried to meet as many of the intelligent and successful persons: teachers, bankers and businessmen. They knew I was very young and was new, and they did not especially care to meet somebody like me. They were the experienced men who had gone through the campaign in France last year and had their friends and established relationships within the unit. I had nothing to offer to them.

One radio troop had a number of soldiers who seemed to be different--irreverent toward the army and particularly toward Lieutenant Hornberg. They also seemed to be very careful and kept to themselves.

One day I happened to go with one of them up to the immense sand dunes near Arcachon at Pyla-sur-mer. His name was Roland Horn. He turned out to be more talkative than I expected. He was about ten years older than I and exhibited a paternal air.

"You are one of those new little Nazi boys, aren't you?" he asked half mockingly.

"Well, not really--"

"You must be. You were brought up that way, all of you. That's all you know, isn't it? But I will tell you..." He panted slightly, somewhat short of breath from trudging uphill through the sand. "It is different than you all think. You know what is going to happen? Why don't you check what Hitler has done so far. He conquered Poland and gave almost half of it to Russia. They did not have to shoot one single bullet.

And then England. England and France always hated each other and have fought many wars, as you know. What happened to the British Expedition Corps? They left! They went back to England, leaving the French high and dry."

"But--" I tried to break in, but he did not let me finish.

"Yes, it is this way. Think of Dunquergue! Will you tell me why Hitler held his troops back? Will you tell me that?"

"Roland, I don't know. But I wondered about that myself."

"My friend, here is the answer. England felt threatened by Germany, but more so by Russia. England can do without France, but needed a strong Germany to protect them and Europe from any Russian attack. And Hitler knew this. He wanted somehow to "preserve" British soldiers: they were Aryans,they were much like Germans. They would help fighting against Russia- - -"

He stopped for a moment, apparently getting short of breath while climbing towards the top of the dune through the deep sand. Then he looked at me:

"You look like somebody who is unsure of himself and is seeking something. . .what are you hunting for, Dietz?"

"I don't really know", I stuttered. I was amazed how well he had read me. " One thing I know is that this war is wrong, that it destroys so much. . . that it is not right to do all this killing. . . we cannot justify it."

"And you volunteered into the armed forces to prove that they all are wrong? You know, that is about as stupid as anyone can be!"

"Yes, maybe. But I wanted to feel the reality of war. And I would have to go to the armed forces anyhow. By volunteering I could at least choose where to go, and not just to the infantry. I did not know how long they would keep this offer open."

"O.k. I see. . . but. . . I guess you could not have waited."

"- - and Roland. . . I want to become a writer. I need life experience. I had to get away from home, for other reasons too.. Don't ask me why. This was my only chance. I know I am stuck with my decision, but everybody says the war will be over in a year or so. I might even find something to write about."

We finally had come to the top of this incredibly high dune, completely out of breath from trudging through the deep sand. We sat down and looked towards the setting sun behind the endless waves of the Bay of Biscay.

Suddenly it came to me: Yes, far behind the horizon, behind the endless waves, was America, a land without Naziism and militarism, a free land. And further to the left there would be South America, the land of the "Golden River", and the Caballeros who wanted to find it and its treasures. . . . . .

Forget about it, Dietz. You are in the German Army, and you are not free. They can do with you whatever they want.

Can they? First some uncomfortable, then more challenging and exciting ideas came to my mind. Yes! Would there be a possibility? America was not at war with us at this time! Dietz, think! You have some relatives in New York!

No, Dietz, you are crazy.

I must have laughed, watching the battle of ideas which took place in my mind.

"What are you thinking about?" Roland brought me back to reality.

"Nothing special, Roland. Lets go back to our quarters. It is getting chilly."

Indeed, the sun had started to hide behind some clouds, and a cool breeze had come up from the bay.

. We got up and returned to the bus stop and went back to Arcachon. In my mind I still could hear the tune and the words of the "Golden River" song. It came on stronger and stronger. Man, find it!

O.k. Dietz, but you also better realize where you are: you are Pvt. Dietz Heller, in the signal corps unit attached to a Tank Corps, don't you know?

Still, Dietz, try it.

Karl Weber came over and told me that we would get two new men, both from Hamburg again. The father of one of them supposedly was the Party Chief of a county...

Oh no. That must be Heinrich von Ellsleben. I thought he was going to be a dive bomber pilot and sink a few British aircraft carriers. That was the way he had talked.

It was Heinrich all right. The air force had refused him because of a chronic middle ear infection. Of all things he was assigned to our troup. He barely said "Hello" to me. He immediately concentrated on Sergeant Bass and made friends with him. Bass was impressed with his father's position.

Those two somehow fit well together. One afternoon they were sitting in Bass's room and sang Nazi songs.

I knew I had to be very careful of what I said or did in Heinrich's presence. Why hadn't they sent him to the Africa Corps or some other distant place?

The other new arrival I did not know. He seemed to be normal and nice and was assigned to troup C.

But Heinrich--I would have him on my neck day and night from now on...

. . .

It was now March 1941. The talk about some great mysterious campaign intensified. Nobody though, knew anything for sure. Staff sergeant Petersen walked around with a gleam in his eyes and annoyed us because he seemed to be so proud to know something we did not know. The officers had one conference after another.

One morning we were washing our all-terrain vehicle. Franz Hesse, the driver, looked gloomy and serious. Something must have happened. I wanted to be friendly and asked him, "Franz, something wrong? You look so...bitter! Can I help you in any way?"

I expected him to tell me to mind my own business or some similar refusal of my offer to help him. Not this time though. Franz came fairly close to me, looked into my eyes. "Dietz", he said, obviously struggling to keep his rage under control, "We are going to invade Russia. Maybe in a month or so. I just can't believe it. Verfluchte Scheisse! Why does he want to do that and break another pact? It is criminal, that's what it is."

I was shocked to see that his hands were shaking.

"Franz! That can't be true. That would be suicide. He will break Germany's neck with that ! Russsia is so big--so endless!" I was trembling too.

"I know, it is hard to believe. But I know that it is true. Mark my words!"

He returned to the front end of the car, where he had been working on the headlights, still obviously furious.

. . .

During the next week all talk centered on a possible transfer to East Prussia. My heart sank into my stomach. Then Franz was right. Oh, no, the rumor mill said, we are going to be sent to Koenigsberg and then put on ships for the invasion of England.

Somebody must think that we were fools.

At the end of March Sergeant Petersen was ordered to take four men along and prepare company quarters somewhere in East Prussia. I was one of the selected ones. First I thought this was an honor, until I realized that the other guys would stay at least one more week here in Arcachon ,in the warm French spring.

Dietz, wake up!

. . .

CHAPTER 16

A bitter cold wind from the east greeted us when we arrived in a small, but well-known garrison town in East Prussia.

Allenstein exemplified everything the name Prussia suggested: army dominance, garrison life, endless maneuvers. The town was full of troops, troops and more troops. Every park hid tanks, artillery pieces and innumerable trucks and army cars. We saw a lot of officers in their all-terrain vehicles, looking serious and very important.

It was still winter here, and we were outright miserable. A pick-up truck brought us to a little desolate village in an area where the first real battle between Russia and Germany had been fought in the First World War.

The people in the village were friendly. However, they had a very strong East Prussian accent and were hard to understand.

We started our job preparing a number of houses by sweeping rooms and stuffing paper sacks with straw to make mattresses.

At night we went to the biggest farmhouse, where you could get additional food. A tall, heavy woman named Mrs. Ackerman did the cooking, using a gigantic frying pan. Everybody stood around while she prepared the food. The room soon smelled to us like heaven: eggs, bacon, fried potatoes.

She was a strong woman. Her husband, like everybody else's, had been drafted, so she ran the farm by herself with the help of her children and some hired men. She had a few Polish prisoners-of-war under her control. Her personality was as strong as her physique, and she did not mind asking us questions.

"What are you all doing here, anyhow? Allenstein and Rastenburg are overflowing with soldiers and all kinds of artillery and tanks. What is going on? You are not thinking of making war against Russia? Oh, yes, you are. I think that is horrible, it is insane. We have gone through this before."

The woman searched for words. For a short minute nobody talked. It was awkward.

One of the soldiers spoke up. "Mrs. Ackerman, we do have a non-aggression pact with Russia. Maybe we all will be shipped somewhere else, or train for the invasion..."

His words died down, killed by the silent and also deadly staring of Master Sergeant Petersen.

The woman then continued with great bitterness.

"You don't know the Russians. They are not well educated at all, and you are smarter than they are, but they will fight. They will defend their country and they will follow their leaders even if they are communists. The one thing we learned in the First World War is that they have great love for Mother Russia. It is much deeper than you think. Maybe it is all they have got, but enough for them to fight."

We saw that she was upset, and we tried to calm her down, but to no avail.

"You men always want to make war. Everybody talks war. Maybe you get killed, and it is all over for you, but who will suffer in the long run? The wives and the children, they will. The wives will do the work, bring up the children, fatherless. I know, because I have seen this happen during the last war. My father was killed on the front, not far from here, and my mother brought us up, all five of us, all by herself. Who talks about us women and the children? All you read about is heroism and medals and the Knight's Cross--for men.

"Oh, it is no use. You will do what you want anyway"

I could see that she was crying. She lifted a part of her large apron and wiped her tears off. Then she hefted the enormous frying pan and slipped the eggs and potatoes on each plate.

None of us soldiers felt like talking. We all ate hastily. We paid for our meal, thanked her and left.

I bit my lip. The woman had been right. I had heard about the great love for Mother Russia that helped the Russians to endure incredible suffering through many years. This love emanated from the beautiful Cosack choirs I had listened to. It almost was a religious power.

"Hitler, stay away from this country, stay away. This attack plan is not going to go well. It might turn out to be a disaster..." The little voice inside of me, first heard in France, had spoken again.

. . .

I still was fretting over the question whether Hitler would really attack Russia, when suddenly more alarming news came over the radio. Rudolf Hess, who was to be Hitler's heir in case of death, had taken one of the newest fighter-bomber planes and flown to England. Hess had been raised in Cairo, where his German parents lived, and then had become Hitler's most devoted follower after he had met him and apparently fallen under his spell.

Had Hess flown to England in order to negotiate a peace settlement? Or was he insane as Hitler declared him to be? Nobody knew or would say anything. The Party wanted us to overlook this affair.

To me this incident seemed to be fishy. How had Hess flown with so much accuracy to the country home of a well-known man, who had been a friend of his years ago? Hess had met the Duke of Hamilton at the Olympic Games in Berlin. Rudolf Hess parachuted and landed less then ten miles away from the estate of the duke.

I was full of questions. This was not a good omen.

I could not talk about this with any of the other guys of our commando. I had to wait until Roland Horn arrived.

After a few days the company rolled in with all the radio trucks, all-terrain vehicles and other trucks and cars.

What was on the front end of every vehicle, though? I gazed at all the neatly rolled-up wooden logs made of the tough hickory wood from southern France, connected with wires. What were they for? I wondered. Ah, yes. We would have to deal with the bad roads in Poland that would be otherwise impassable after any lengthy rain.

Impassable roads in Poland...and in Russia!

I found Roland. We walked over to an area where nobody could hear us, away from the farmhouses. You had to be very careful when you wanted to talk freely. Get out of range of the other men. Roland appeared to be nervous and depressed.

"Dietz, I am glad that we can talk. Hitler will attack Russia. It makes me sick. Now he is breaking another holy promise, and this time he is really playing with fire. Just think how huge and endless Russia is!"

Yes, I know. Despite everything they say Russia is an awesome power. I feel...I think it is going to be a deadly mistake. He is biting off too much, and he breaks his word--again."

"Remember when we talked about England using Germany as a bulwark against Russia? Here we are. They won their gamble, they have it made now. And we--we have lost, no matter what."

I had to leave though, and we both said that we should get together soon again.

. . .

The following afternoon I thought I had to do something, or make some decision about everything, if I could.

I went to the little schoolhouse, where I knew I could be alone for a while. The children had left for the day.

I brought a bottle of Steinhaeger schnapps with me. I had been told that you never should drink alone, but this was different. I knew that I probably would have nobody to confide in for a long time. Maybe Roland Horn. I took a long drink, then settled at the teacher's desk and drank some more.

Poland, Norway, Denmark, then the Netherlands, Belgium and France...then the Balkan States. Where was the promise Hitler made after he entered Czechoslovakia that he did not have any further territorial demands in Europe? It was just another lie of this man.

The criminal decision to attack Russia was plainly attempted robbery on a tremendously large scale. This was not even revenge for past injustice anymore. He was now trying to grab innumerable square miles of Russian land, maybe even all of Russia. He was like Attila the Hun, but in reverse direction, or like Genghis Khan.

The Steinhaeger must have hit me at this time. I laughed to myself. Attila the Hun in reverse--I thought that was very clever.

Keep allegiance to this man? No. No.

"But Dietz", my little voice chimed in, "you are in the German army! How can you expect not to obey their orders? You know what they will do to you, without even hesitating!"

Yes, but there has to be a way. I have the right and the duty to protect myself against a leadership that does not know right from wrong--morally.

You've got a problem, Dietz.

Passive resistance? Yes, that was the word. I had to try that. Do what you really have to do, but not more than that, look for an opening somewhere. There had to be one. Do not do the things you had sworn not to do--remember that afternoon at Wolf's house, with Wolf there and Signe witnessing our pact? Stay decent!

Yes. I would try that. I would fight for that, for my integrity. Nobody wanted to die in a war, but I certainly did not want to die for them--the Nazi leaders and the ambitious generals.

Despite the hopelessness of the situation I now felt much more confident, even a little adventurous. Yes, this would be a tough challenge, may a real adventure.

I closed the bottle of Steinhaeger and started to walk back to my quarters. As I crossed the school yard I caught myself whistling the tune about the Golden River, the song I had started to love when I was at the shore of the Baltic Sea, the song about those men in Brazil dreaming of a golden future, Caballeros, who enjoyed their freedom more than anything else. Freedom, independence for my own life - - yes, I remembered the song so well..

" Let's go, men, let's go and find the golden river!"

Yes, I would somehow, and I would keep my integrity intact. No matter what. It now was serious business.

BOOK TWO

Heller's Hell

CHAPTER 17

Within a day everything changed drastically. The whole company sprung into action. The master sergeant announced that we would move tomorrow to the border of the Russian-occupied zone of Poland. That was it then! Oh brother,-thats all I could say.

My head was spinning, my mind went far away. what could I do?. That was stupid, that was treacherous, that would have a horrible end! Think of Napoleon and his debacle! How Moscow burned and turned his troops back!

I could not do anything, I had to execute the orders given to me. Cars and trucks were checked, gasoline was distributed , rifles and ammunition were checked. I had a sleepless night and tossed and turned.

We started to roll eastwards early in the morning on June 21, 1941. Karl Weber and I were sitting in the radio truck in front of the transmitters and receivers. We had strict orders not to transmit anything whatsoever.

On the left side of the road were railroad tracks. One train after another passed, crammed with vehicles, tanks, and artillery, all of them rolling eastwards.

The road now became much too narrow to accommodate all the trucks and cars. Finally the drivers just went off the road, right and left, and drove through the endless wheat fields in complete disregard for the crops. Tanks, trucks, cars and artillery pieces pulled by heavy tractors were rolling six to eight vehicles abreast, stirring up an immense dust cloud that must have been visible for miles.

Karl and I still did not feel like talking. All this was so wrong, so stupid, dangerous and ill conceived, no matter how many tanks or artillery pieces or trains with equipment and ammunition we saw. I remembered fragments of a song we had learned sometime ago, written by a cavalry soldier of a doomed battalion, who realized that they were riding into their certain peril, not being able to do anything about it.

Dust crept into our radio truck, and we had to clean the equipment every so often with a rag. We even had to fashion facemasks for ourselves using handkerchiefs.

Suddenly a terrific roaring noise came from above. We cranked our heads out of the windows. Squadron after squadron of bombers, dive-bombers and fighter planes filled the air with an incredibly loud sound. They had to fly very low in order to escape enemy radar.

We made innumerable stops. Commands were shouted. The air was filled with suffocating gasoline and diesel fumes.

This was the mighty German army rolling east with all its power: a fearsome display of military might. They had created their own "Rollbahn," a tremendously wide "road " on which it moved,crushing miles of crops on its unholy mission.

On the frequent stops Karl and I went out of the radio truck and talked with other soldiers.

"This is different, guys, different than the day we entered France," one of the older soldiers said, "Nobody is excited about this. I am not, I tell you that. The whole thing is somehow--irrealistic." And another man said "I think it is plainly rotten. I thought we were going to deal with Russia rather than attack her. They are too big for us." He looked carefully right and left. You could not say something like that in front of officers.

It was obvious that there was no spirit, no enthusiasm at all. And the army would go into Russia and kill and destroy a land which had not provoked her.

In the late afternoon the lead vehicle, Captain Schultz's armored troop carrier, suddenly turned off the road onto a small dirt path--you could not even call it a road. We followed his vehicle through a rather dense forest until he stopped at a place where the forest opened up onto a large meadow. We parked our vehicles under the trees and immediately camouflaged them.

Most of us felt sullen and moody; we dreamed about getting out of here, going home or getting back to France. In the distance we could hear the continuous rumble of the thousands of vehicles on the rollbahn, going east.

At 9 p.m. they whistled and shouted for roll call. We all lined up at the edge of the meadow so we could run for cover if planes should appear.

Lieutenant Hornberg, the haughty company commander, now started to read an edict by the Fuehrer to his soldiers.

"Tomorrow morning the German forces are going to invade the Soviet Union, the arch enemy of Germany since communism has taken over. Germany's destination always has been the East. We need "Lebensraum", space for our population. The Soviet Republic will be conquered in a few weeks. Revolution will spring up in Russia and that will help our cause. The Russians are ready to throw away the communistic rule."

Then came the worst, and what would give this edict the infamous name of the "Commissar"s order: "It will be a different and harsh war, a fight for life and death. No weakness like tolerance or mercy was going to be allowed. All political commissars would be shot or handed over to the officers."

And then of all things those words: "God the Almighty will be with us."

What blasphemy.

Even Lieutenant Hornberg had stopped from time to time, looking at Captain Schultz for approval and reassurance. To his credit I must say that Hornberg was embarrassed by what he had to read.

But Captain Schultz looked straight ahead and did not blink an eye. No guts, no signs of disgust--no opinion. "Just swallow this incredible edict," his posture read. "It is the Fuehrer's will. Amen."

And not one man spoke up. No one. We all felt as if we had been railroaded. I did not speak up either. We have a pact with Russia! How can this happen? My mind screamed, but I remained silent like all the other guys.

Hornberg had finished. Most soldiers looked as if they did not believe what they just heard. What happened to the spirit of Prussia, the proud army with its supposedly strict code of ethics? Hitler had ordered to kill all the commissars? Unbelievable!

Hitler had betrayed us. He had broken the pact with Soviet Russia. He had now turned around 180 degrees and was going to attack her.

It was a desperate feeling to be now a victim of his broken promise. His obvious brutality and the stupid, greedy decision made me sick. You can't beat Russia. I felt that Russia was endless and would provide millions of soldiers, more than we ever could have.

I made up my mind: I was not obligated to follow this man and his clique of militaristic crooks, I was justified to find my own way out of this mess.

Suddenly I thought of the song of the Brazilian Caballeros:
"Let's go, men, lets go and find the golden river…" Now I changed it to
: "Go, man, go and find the golden river!" Sure, this was an allegoric river,
which meant to me not real gold, but life in freedom, and independence,
being my own master, wherever I wanted to be. And the tune sounded
catchy to me, stimulating.

I had found my own battle cry.

When the company was dismissed, the soldiers were slow to leave.
Everybody seemed to try to find somebody with whom he could share his
anger.

Hitler also had broken his holy promise not to open a second front.

Not everybody was depressed, though. Heinrich Bass was whistling. He
behaved like somebody who was looking forward to a time where promotion
and maybe a decoration could be in the books. He enthusiastically gave
orders to us to check the radio sets, the generator and the antennas -
everything.

He saw me when I cleaned my rifle. He halted in front of me.
"Radioman Heller, do a good job," he said, "It will be real war now, and
even you might have to use your rifle, like a good German soldier."

Master Sergeant Petersen strutted around, and his body motions
reminded me a lot of Benito Mussolini with his peacock-like walk. "Didn't
I tell you so, guys?" he said triumphantly to Georg Osten and me. "This
is going to be a great campaign."

Told us so? He never had said one word.

Georg Osten was called to see Sergeant Bass, but now Karl Weber
came back with two canisters of gasoline. He was perspiring profusely. I
knew how heavy they were, I had carried some myself earlier. Karl's face
was pale, but not from physical exhaustion; he clearly looked worried to
me.

"Karl, this is horrible." I dared to say, "What do you think?"

Karl looked into the distance, still in a state of shock. "Dietz, what
is going to happen? Are we going to shoot all commissars? What about
-- decency and honor?"

I embraced him shortly without saying a word. I knew now that I was
not alone in this mess. I would have at least one guy around who felt like
I did.

And I needed that: Sergeant Bass told us that Heinrich von Ellsleben
definitely had been assigned to our troup. He replaced Heinz Kerle, who
suddenly was assigned to the wireless repair shop.

We took some blankets from our truck and just lay down for the night. I believe nobody really slept. I said good-bye to happiness and any future plans -- and wished I had the guts to run away and escape to Bremerhaven and to the USA.

At dawn the German artillery opened up and started to hit Russian forces. The war was on.

A little later the officers told us that the Russians were completely surprised. At six a.m. we got into our cars and trucks and started to roll towards the main road. A little Russian RATA biplane flew over the forest and dropped a few bombs far away from us. Then we were on the highway, driving through Lithuania in an endless column of cars, tanks and artillery.

The RATA plane had not scared me. The bombs had fallen far away. It just was a strange feeling to see for the first time the "enemy", even if it was a plane that did not do us any harm.

But driving into the Russian-held Lithuanian country was a very strange feeling: a mixture of objection, guilt and of a strong premonition of coming disaster.

Our radio truck had a roof antenna. We could send and receive messages while driving. Motorcycle messengers came and handed us messages, or came to receive others. We established a connection between the headquarters of a squadron of observation planes and the Panzerkorps. Coding, decoding, transmitting and receiving: the capacity of our receivers and the transmitter was stretched to the limit within a few hours. Our own war had started.

We were told that General Hoth, our army commander, would make an inspection of the troops as we rolled east.

There he was, standing at the side of the road, all by himself. His adjutant stood respectfully placed ten feet behind him. General Hoth's uniform was spotless, his boots were shiny. How could that be in this road dust? The Knight's Cross was dangling from his neck. He looked very serious, strict and detached, in a world of his own -- the typical Prussian officer.

Georg Osten and I were sitting next to each other in front of our radio sets. Both of us stared at the general. I could not stop myself from saying, "Hey, Georg, there is one of your special friends, a real Prussian general, immaculate even in this dusty mess."

"You know," George said, "I prefer our General Schmitt. He is right up here near the front and sometimes is as dirty as we are. He even goes in with the tanks, if he wants to know more. He did this already in the French campaign, and I understand he is doing the same here. He is a man of my taste: he lives a life like we do, and not the damned life of a figurehead." I knew what he meant.

One of our frequencies was almost identical to radio Moscow's wavelength. Even as we were on telegraphy and Radio Moscow was on telephony, their signal was so strong that it almost completely blocked out our messages, and we had to repeat them again and again. Every half hour they played the Russian anthem, the "Internationale," and we just as well could have shut down during that time.

The first big town in Lithuania was Vilnius. We somehow had to stay on the city square, putting our regular antennas up.In the morning, as Karl Weber and I were tending the sets, a few Russian planes appeared from nowhere, flying very low, so low that I could see the face of one of their pilots. They threw their bombs, and for a few seconds hell seemed to have broken loose.

Karl and I had to jump out of the radio truck and fling ourselves to the ground - without having time to take the earphones off. I felt a hard jolt, and my head jerked back hard.

Sergeant Bass had seen us. This was food for his ego, and he made a few uncomplimentary remarks about "us high school boys not being so smart after all." There was much excitement about the air raid, but nothing serious had happened, and we forgot about it fast.

We returned to our radio sets.

A little later Karl suddenly pulled on my arm sleeve. "Listen, Dietz!" He was really excited. "Go on my frequency." I did. There it was: "Dinah, is there anyone finer, in the State of Carolina..." Both of us could not believe it. Here, in Lithuania, American songs? While they had been banned in Germany for years? Did the people here ,under Soviet regime, have more freedom than we had in Nazi Germany? I wondered.

Later on Karl or I checked the same station again and again. They still were playing only one song, all morning long. "Dinah..."

Again we joined the endless columns of infantry, artillery and some tanks, all of them moving eastward. The infantrymen now seemed to look so tired and exhausted, fighting the dust created by all the vehicles on the frequently unpaved roads, and heat and the billions of mosquitoes.

The following day we reached Bjelo-Russia, the most western part of the Soviet Union. There was no turning around anymore. As a matter of fact, a staff officer we knew from our air force connection, stood at the bridge and waved our truck over. "Soldiers, do you know what the name of this little river is?"

A pitiful little creek was flowing under the bridge.

"That is the Beresina, and don't you remember from school? This is the exact spot where Napoleon crossed into Russia in 1812. You know what happened to him and the French army, but I will tell you: we will be in Moscow in four weeks, we will be all done before the winter comes. We have a big Swastika flag in our trunk, and we will hoist it over the Kremlin!"

This Captain always tried to teach us something, whenever he had a chance to talk with us.

The Beresina was a small creek with brownish water, flowing slowly to the north. Napoleon -- I had seen enough pictures of his devastated army trying to flee back to the west through murderous snow and ice, after the Russians had burned Moscow.

Other officers stopped by our radio truck regularly. We came to know most of them.

On the seventh day of the invasion an air force colonel approached. He was the new intelligence and information officer. We liked him immediately because he was bright, friendly and not aloof and knew how to get along with plain soldiers. He always seemed to be very knowledgeable, but on this day he also seemed to be very worried about something. He shifted his weight from one foot to another as he waited for an immediate answer to one of the messages he had brought.

"Boys, I don't know," he finally said. "Something is not right. Every time we take prisoners and interrogate them, we find out that they belong to new divisions of which we had no knowledge. They come from mid-Russia and from points East. We are surprised, to say the least. The Russians seem to have almost twice as many divisions as we thought. How is that possible? Why did we not know about this? Intelligence has failed us completely."

We listened with some terror. If that was true? The colonel reached in his pocket and brought up a pack of cigarettes, took one out and lit it himself, before we could get our matches ready. Then he continued.

"And their tanks are so much better than ours, especially the T34. Our antitank guns don't even dent their armor, our shells just pop off into the air. The only advantage we have is that they do not keep their tanks in good condition and waste a lot by not having well trained crews. They do not have good repair facilities and have a lot of breakdowns. Our antiaircraft

88 batteries fortunately are very good at blowing their tanks to smithereens - but we do not have that many batteries here.

"Another thing: the number of their tanks is just unbelievable. Their factories are far East, beyond the Ural mountains, where we cannot get to them. Man, if I had known all this..."

The colonel looked around nervously, then he continued his report.

"They know how to disappear, tanks, artillery, and all. They suddenly are gone into the forests, and we cannot find them. I am sorry to have to tell you all this. To me it looks as if we will never get them. We are in trouble. Our intelligence has failed us completely."

By then Sergeant Bass had finished decoding the message the colonel was waiting for, and he handed him the paper. The colonel thanked him and walked away slowly, and I noticed that he shook his head a few times.

Karl and I slumped at our radio sets. After he had left neither of us could say a word.

Another alarming fact was that Hitler let the war go on for a week without telling the German people any details about the campaign. That was strange and certainly not a good omen.

. . .

Chapter 18

The air now was full of Russian planes. We called them "Martin" bombers. Supposedly they were of American design. Their engines had a high-pitched, whining sound and you never would mistake these planes for other types. The German fighter planes shot them down easily by getting behind them. They had no rear gunner.

Again a group of these bombers appeared on the sky. They tried to fly from one cumulus cloud to another to stay covered. but a few Messerschmitts found them and shot three planes down within minutes.

We looked on as seven parachutes appeared and slowly drifted down. Suddenly I heard a sound that first resembled popcorn popping. Then I realized it was rapid firing from hundreds of rifles. The infantry had started shooting at the helpless men hanging in their parachutes. How could they do that! That was barbaric! They were over German-held territory! There was no need to kill them!

I gritted my teeth and must have said something like "Oh, my God, these guys are completely helpless..." as I stared at this spectacle.

Karl Weber felt the same anger. "They can't do that, for heaven's sake!"

We were too far away and could not see whether these men were hit or not. Rudolf Stange, a tall, blond guy from the third radio troop, came over. "I can't believe this. It is horrible! What is going on?"

Nobody could answer this question, but Staff Sergeant Petersen happened to pass by and noticed our anger. He nodded in his patronizing way. "Yes, boys, this is war. You might as well get used to it."

Later that afternoon we came to a large compound near Minsk, apparently a former base for Soviet troops. We saw row after row of barracks, all surrounded with barbed wire fences, large storage sheds and many airplane hangars. After we parked the vehicles and put the antenna up it did not take long until one of the younger liaison officers came over to our truck. He gave us a few messages and wanted to wait for an answer to one of them.

As he was standing there, waiting, he started to talk.

"Men, do you know what this base was used for until a few years ago?"

"No, Herr Leutnant, we don't know." I answered.

"Well, I will tell you," he said while lighting a cigarette, "This base was used as a training camp for German and Russian pilots--yes, German and Russian. The experienced German fighter pilots from the First World War came here to teach the Russians dog fight techniques and all the tricks they had learned. They used whatever planes they could find, and the Russians were very thankful. You know," he scratched the back of his head and grinned, "There was a secret agreement between the German Reichswehr, that is General Seeckt, and the Russians. Germany was not allowed to have an air force on her own, according to the Treaty of Versailles. Well, this way we had plenty of pilots when Hitler created the new German air force in 1935; they were ready to go."

He took a few drags on his cigarette. "But that is not all. Not far from here is a development center for tanks, and--you expect this by now--German and Russian engineers developed and tested tanks, and good ones! I tell you, their T34 tank is far superior to what we have to offer. I understand that engineers in Germany now are working night and day to find a similarly good design. Man, and think of the big Russian T52 tank, even heavier and better protected yet..."

He kept on talking, but I did not want to listen any more. I had heard enough. Karl Weber and Georg Osten kept on listening, though.

What did he say about cooperation between Russian and German militarists, weapon manufacturers and so on? Where was loyalty, dedication to your own fatherland? Was everything a big show, I mean the talk about patriotism and fatherland and so on? Were these guys playing with us, using us as fodder for their battles or their greed for money or power?

I talked with Karl about that, later on, after the lieutenant had left.

"Karl, you know, maybe we all are being fooled. Maybe there is cooperation between those powers, if there are those militaristic manipulators, who do everything illegal they can think of, as long as it gives them a chance to do their work... Didn't some German officers go to China after World War I and build up their army? Didn't Storm Troopers leader Ernst Roehm work for some South American country and organizerd their forces there?"

"Yes," Karl said, "That is true. I also know that they secretly built parts of submarines in Finland and Spain and shipped them to Kiel for assembly. What other dirty deals were going on?"

He stopped for a minute. Then he continued.

"On the other hand, Germany got a bad deal in Versailles. No air force, a very small amount of troops, no battle ships. I don't know. What is right?"

"Karl, it is not what is right. It is what are we stuck with! What can we do about all this?"

What a dangerous gamble the whole campaign was anyway. A few days of rain would have stopped almost everything. All roads were in horrible condition. They were just plain dirt roads. In all Western Russia we saw only one acceptable road; the one from Smolensk towards Moscow.

Right now red dust, stirred up by the thousands of vehicles, filled the air day and night. When the moon came up it had a strong reddish color.

Well, wasn't that romantic? But as big and weird as the red moon was, I could not bring up any spirit of romance, not even of adventure. Too much bad news had been brought to us, and I could not forget what the officers had told us.

A few minutes earlier a twin engine plane had cruised around here and the pilot had spotted the general's adjutant. He had waved a big flag. The plane then swooped down very low and dropped a container very close to the adjutant--probably with some important messages in it. They are pretty well organized, I thought.

I sat on the hood of our radio truck and looked at the big red moon. Every so often a breeze brought some cool air from a nearby lake.

Of all things a little rhyme came to my mind. I had read it some years ago. It was from a story of a German prisoner-of-war in World War I who had escaped the camp and was on his way back to the fatherland, walking at night and hiding in the forests in daytime. This man had seen the red moon too, probably at harvest time.

"Ich trank mit meiner Base
auf Du und Du,
der Mond mit roter Nase

Sah zu, sah zu."
(A distant cousin and me
wanted to drop the impersonal "Sie".
So, we switched to "Du" doing some drinking
'Til the red-nosed moon seemed to be blinking.)

Sure, this was a silly little poem, but it fit somehow the time and the place. The whole world seemed to be crazy anyway.

The pace was hectic, the work load was overwhelming. No mail had come since we had invaded Russia, and honestly, we really hardly had any time to think of home.

We were close to a city called Witebsk on our way to Moscow. The fighting had intensified, and the Russian's seemed to put up much more resistance. The talk was that now some crack divisions from the Moscow area were involved. Artillery fire rumbled in the distance day and night. Sometimes a few rounds were fairly close. For a while dive-bombers attacked a certain area again and again.

We set up our radio station a few miles away from the main road. For some reason we were close to the general's tent.

Nothing seemed to be right from the beginning. First it was persistent rifle fire from a nearby forest, then a few rounds of grenade throwers were sent in our direction from the woods. Maybe there were some partisans or other troops in the forest. The general did not like it and had us call an observation plane.

After ten minutes the plane arrived and started to cruise over the forest. One of the adjutants came over and made us switch to telephony so we could make contact with the plane. Usually it was strictly forbidden to do that since everybody believed the Russians could intercept us easily.

The adjutant was given the first set, and I had the second headset on and listened in.

"Herr Oberleutnant, something is going on in those woods. I cannot see well and I am asking permission to descend five-hundred feet." We could see the plane well as it was circling over the forest.

"Permission granted, Lieutenant, but leave immediately if there is trouble!"

The plane dropped a few hundred feet. Suddenly hell broke loose as the whole forest turned into a rifle range. Then several machine guns joined in.

The pilots voice came in. "I got some hits--probably in the engine." He sounded pretty calm.

"Get out of there, man, get out, Lieutenant!"

We could see the plane banking and turning to our area. But the pilot's voice clearly sounded distressed when he called in again.

"The engine is hit, we are losing power...we have to abort...it is an emergency!"

"Lieutenant, not here, get further away...you know why!"

"I don't know whether I can...we will try...no, I have to put her down right now...over and out."

The plane tried to get away from the area where the general's tent was, but could not quite make it. It barely cleared a hedge and then touched down, rumbling over a very rough and uneven stretch of pretty high grass.

Pilot and navigator jumped out of the plane and ran over to our radio truck. Both were excited. "Get out of here, as soon as you can! The whole forest is full of troops and tanks. Get out before they start moving!"

I had tried during the pilot-officer conversation to write a few important points down. Now I started to run over to the General's adjutant to give him that information.

Suddenly somebody came from behind me, grabbed the papers and ran with them to the adjutant, who looked very curious at this scene.

It was Heinrich. That son of a bitch. He screamed: "Herr Leutnant! Here is all the important conversation!" The adjutant took the papers, did not even thank him, and disappeared in the general's tent.

If there ever was a rotten act played on me, that was it. I was furious. I held my temper, though, and I knew I would seek revenge for that.

Within a few minutes we were ordered to get ready, put the antennas down, start the cars and trucks.

We lined up on a very small dirt road. One single Russian antitank gun shot a shell every twenty seconds from the direction of the forest, uncomfortably close for our taste. The general had called for a company of infantry on motorcycles. They now arrived from the west, drove around us or used the dried -out ditch to move towards the forest. Shortly thereafter we heard their machine guns pouring bullets into the woods.

Karl was sitting on my right side. That's where the antitank gunfire came from. He wanted some kind of protection. He started to dismantle the transmitter to make something to shield him.

"Karl, you cannot do that! That won't protect you anyhow! It is nothing but aluminum and wires and tubes!" I yelled.

"I can do it, and I will do it. It is better than nothing at all. Why don't you sit on my side?"

If it had not been such a serious situation, I could have laughed my head off. But Karl was right. He finished dismantling the transmitter and held it against the window. And he was happy.

There was a very decrepit wooden bridge holding us up, but finally we made it to the main road. For the first time we had to drive in a westerly direction. That was a very strange feeling, but probably did not mean anything.

We came to a little village. In the center of it there were many officers and sergeants of the field gendarmerie surrounding a small group of Russian prisoners. All we could see were the heads of the prisoners, most of them dark-haired. This was something unusual and we could not figure what was going on.

Half an hour later we finally stopped and put our antenna up at the new location. After a while one of the liaison officers came by. "Soldiers, do you know what all this excitement was, a few miles back, with those prisoners in the middle of that village? You would not believe it, but Stalin's son Jacob was one of them, and other officers of his unit. They belonged to a crack Moscow tank division, the one that was hiding in the forest. They had heavy losses from dive bomber attacks and were regrouping."

I wished I had been sure which one of the prisoners actually was Jacob, Stalin's son. They all looked alike to me.

Not to Heinrich, though. He crowed "That was him, the one with the smooth hair! I know for sure!" He was all excited.

Georg Osten had his number by now. He coolly said: "Could be, Heinrich. How many times have you met him?"

This was an obvious defeat. Heinrich did not take it lightly. He stammered for a few seconds, then he said, "You all don't know anything or anybody. Just read your newspapers, and you will know more. My father will..."

He stopped immediately. Then he buried himself into some instruction manual.

And I was determined to take revenge for what he had done earlier when he grabbed the message away. But how?

Altogether this was not our day. One message after another needed to be sent, others were received. No food came through, no coffee or other liquids. Finally we had to talk Sergeant Bass into letting us use part of our emergency rations.

"You want us to continue to work, don't you?" Georg Osten said. "You don't want us to fall asleep on the sets?" Finally Bass gave in and let us use half of our high-energy, caffeine rich patties. Our hearts started to beat wildly from the caffeine, but somehow we felt very important.

Bass had refused to eat the patties. I asked George whether we should look for a halo around Bass's head. He laughed.

The words of the colonel who had told us about the poor service our intelligence had provided kept echoing in my mind. Everything was now suspicious: all the new graves we saw at the side of the road, the lack of the announced hundreds of thousands of prisoners who supposedly were going west on the main road, also the lack of the thousands of captured tanks or artillery pieces...maybe the divisional headquarters were not reporting truthfully.

Even worse was the news that our attack on Moscow was to be diverted to the south. Moscow...some of our advance units already had been in the suburbs of the city.

The Ukraine, the breadbasket of Russia, was the main target now. Wheat, potatoes, and in the southern part you would be close to oil.

Fast victory,though, was slipping away. The first leaves were falling, and the winter was not far away. We were not going to make it this year.

All of a sudden our unit was put on a train and sent up north towards Leningrad.

We settled down in a surprisingly clean village, with much nicer houses than we had ever seen. We even saw a few flowers here and there. The talk was that Finnish people had been living here.

However, no action was in progress as far as the city was concerned. Some soldiers claimed to have seen spires of churches in Leningrad, when they climbed up an observation platform.

No action. That was a great letdown. I started to brood about everything; the war, the future. Karl Weber handled it much better. He constantly wrote something down like what kind of meals we had, how many cigarettes he had exchanged for vitamin pills, and how much money he had saved from his salary.

Mail caught up with us. I had several letters, one of them from Signe. I noticed that my hands were trembling when I opened it. Come on, now, Dietz. Take it easy.

Signe wrote that her parents had decided to go back to Sweden and had applied for the necessary papers. She herself did not feel like going, but she was not sure. She also said that Wolf was in a hospital in Bremerhaven with some medical disease. This was going to interrupt his schedule, and he thought that he might have to start all over with the next class. Then she wanted to know how I took everything. Whether I had suffered any injuries...whether I had time to think of her and whether I had looked at her pictures on and off. I almost could hear her chuckle when I read that. No, there was no better girl in the world than her.

Wolf wrote too, telling me about his sickness, and that he still had high hopes to get over it soon. Another letter was from Nolle, and I had to laugh out loud when I read his story: a friend of ours, Fritz Detweiler, and he had installed a P.A. system loudspeaker on top of the school roof and played the sound of an air raid siren just about the time when the big mathematics examination was to take place. Everybody went to the air raid shelter, and the examination had to be canceled. Even better than that; when they removed the speaker the next day, Mr. Eppler caught them. He broke out in almost hysterical laughter and even helped them to get their sets out of the school.

But I fell back to my brooding. I was thinking about the coming winter. When they announced that the staff was going to play a movie in a large barn, I did not want to go.

Georg Osten shook his head. "Dietz, don't be a fool. Let one of us older guys stay here and watch the radio sets. You need a break, more than anybody else. You are getting too serious."

"Thanks, Georg, I know what you mean. But I'd rather stay here."

While I was watching our call-in frequency, Roland Horn strolled over to our radio truck. He again smiled his usual all-knowing smile, but this time it was tinged with despair.

"Hi, Dietz, how are you. No, I won't call you "Nazi boy" anymore, don't worry. By the way I guess I have been right with my predictions."

"Yes, Roland, you were. And Hitler's talk about getting us out of here before the winter--that was pure nonsense."

"Man, I cannot see any solution, any chance for victory. I believe we will grind ourselves to death slowly."

Both of us were silent for a while. Then Roland sighed heavily. "Let's get together from time to time and talk, Dietz. I have to go now. See you."

He walked slowly back to his radio truck. I knew what he was thinking.

Finally I caught myself. All this worrying did not help because I could not change anything. Just stay alert. My chance would come.

. . .

CHAPTER 19

Then the rains came. The roads became impassable; they had turned into an almost bottomless morass. The airforce was grounded since there were no hard-surfaced runways. The pioneers built "rollbahnen", made of thousands and thousands of logs, lain side by side. Any tank or heavy vessel would scramble the logs hopelessly and make the road useless. It was a sad spectacle to see the infantrymen whip their horses to pull the heavy field kitchens through all this mess.

Not only rain. The fall season turned out to be extremely short. After just a few weeks the wind became ice cold. It blew incessantly. And with anger we realized that the winter had already come. We were far north.

We were not prepared, neither mentally nor physically. We had no warm clothes, no warm gloves or headgear. Within a few days the infantry soldiers tied straw around their boots, made scarfs from whatever they could find and kept their hands deep in their pockets. They looked like a gang of perfectly disorganized men, but the officers could not say anything. They did the same, maybe in a less conspicuous manner. Within a few days there were many reports of soldiers being ill with pneumonia, and then the endless list of frostbites started.

The drivers could not start their engines in the morning. They tried to place hubcaps with diesel oil under the engines, ignited them in the hope to warm up the engines. A few trucks burned up.

We stood guard night after night, staring into the darkness, facing the merciless, biting wind and drifting snow. The partisans came unseen at night, started fires or threw grenades, and then were swallowed up by the dark.

There was one bright light in this growing misery. A new air force liaison officer, Lieutenant LeClaire, started to come over to our station. He had come fresh from the officer's school in Berlin and belonged to one of the Huguenot families who had fled France during the revolution and settled in Berlin. He turned out to be a refined and enjoyable person ,much more than the average Prussian officer. His uniform always was in immaculate condition. and he wore some kind of a scarf around his neck to protect him from the cold, showing that he had a somewhat independent mind. He was cleanly shaven and always smelled good, using a refreshing eau de cologne. We appreciated this very much, since there always was a somewhat sour smell in a Russian hut.

LeClaire was so much more a uniformed civilian than a strict professional officer. He had verve and imagination, talked about a beautiful future and overall brought an atmosphere of pleasantness and civilization with him whenever he came.

But one afternoon he came over to our station, showing visible distress. "Men, I had some bad news a while ago. One of our observation planes was shot down. One of the crew got out and was seen coming down on his parachute.

I wanted to get a search party together, but the boss said no. He said he could not risk twenty men for one pilot."

"Lieutenant, I am afraid the Russians..." Sergeant Bass stopped just in time. I knew what he was going to say. LeClaire had not heard him. "I knew both of them, the pilot and the navigator. They are fine men, excellent officers. Well, never mind.

Here are some messages. Would you send them right away, please?"

He left then. We felt sorry for him. He probably would find out in a few weeks what really was going on here at the front. No mercy...

A few days later he came over again. This time he did not have any good news either.

"Men, you will not believe this. We have always directed our artillery fire from our observation planes, but now we cannot even find the impact area of the shells. They are easily half a mile off their targets. Why? Because it is so cold, and our guns are not calibrated for these temperatures. It takes half an hour or so to adjust the distances,that is after the gun barrels have warmed up enough. And then," he wiped his forehead. It was hot inside our hut. "...the Russians have built a railroad across the frozen Lake Ladoga and also a truck route. They are supplying Leningrad with a lot of goods.

In daytime we shoot these transportation routes to pieces, but at night they rebuild them somewhere else."

Week by week I could see his enthusiasm crumble. But he himself remained the nicest guy I could imagine, still holding onto his chivalrous views.

We had to handle the daily reports of losses of manpower. It was staggering to see how many soldiers had to be sent back with severe frostbite or pneumonia. Who could stand this weather anyhow? How many more losses could we take? Georg Osten looked over my shoulder and said, "You better not let the Russians see all those figures. They might get ideas." He was not joking.

Would we have to retreat? Would our front hold up? Fortunately the United States was not in the war, and Japan probably kept a good amount of Russian forces from coming here. Maybe everything will be contained, we thought. Maybe it would all be settled next year.

But it was not to be. Suddenly a maximum alert was issued. The Russians had started a powerful offensive on December the sixth. They had brought up many troops from the deep hinterland and from Siberia, well trained and well equipped with winter gear and winter uniforms. They were making progress around Moscow. We had to pack our equipment and be ready to leave within twenty minutes if needed.

One day later the Japanese bombed Pearl Harbor. The Americans had been attacked and they would fight back. They would fight a justifiable war. To be in a war was bad enough, I thought, but psychologically it was a hundred times worse to be in a war that you knew was wrong, the war we started breaking a pact that our "leader" had made.

And it was not just Pearl Harbor. For years the United States had warned Japan to stop her aggressive behavior in Asia, like attacking China years ago.

Hitler then made an incomprehensible mistake. The pact with Japan did not require him to do so, but a power-drunk Hitler now declared war on the United States in a pompous way. He said that he easily could handle a "degenerate nation" with an "alcoholic president" who seemed to be in failing health". Did he think he had a hundred million soldiers and unlimited supplies? This was stupid and suicidal, I thought. Did we not have our hands already full with whatever we had started? Why had Hitler been so careful as not to antagonize the United States all these years, giving us hope that he would not have to fight them - and now he had messed everything up for good.

I had a lot of mixed feelings. I thought of my grandmother and her brothers and her sister in New York, who so generously had supported her all these years. Now they were supposed to be enemies? What nonsense.

Most of the other guys did not seem to care and believed Hitler's words, who said that by the time the United States would be actively engaged in this war we would have conquered Russia and invaded England. All radio stations said this, and they suddenly also engaged in long dissertations describing the Americans as being spoiled and not having the will to fight.

Well, Mr. Eppler - and Roland Horn - here we are. You were so right, and so was my fear, I thought.

I felt that the situation had become hopeless. The Americans had decided the last war, and they would decide this one too.

Despite everything the Christmas holidays were quiet. We had moved to a different village and now were right on the highway to Moscow. Half a mile down the road was a "Dacha", a country home that once belonged to the Czar's family. It was like a large wooden castle. It was interesting to see that our general staff always found some large country estate home or a castle and made them their headquarters, even here in the Soviet Union.

In front of our hut there was heavy traffic on the highway. Trucks, cars and half-tracks were trying to manage the road, which was covered by a heavy layer of ice and snow.

On New Year's Eve Lieutenant LeClaire came over to our hut. He had a few drinks and was in a great mood. Heinrich Bass found the cognac, which he had saved for an occasion like that. After a short while everybody relaxed. LeClaire was telling stories, one after another.

Suddenly he looked at his watch. "Men, it is time! It is time to go outside and have a parade on the road to Moscow! Let's get ready!"

What a crazy idea - but we might as well have fun. We put our caps and coats on. It was twenty-five degrees Celsius below zero, but we did not feel the cold thanks to the cognac.

By now it was dark. Lieutenant LeClaire was in great spirits; "Okay, men, line up here. Right march, face east towards Moscow. Let's start parading! Get your legs up!" We entwined our arms and started high stepping towards Moscow. We sang the tune of an old Prussian march, and as we did not know the words after a while, we just invented some.

Our goose step was pitiful. We had not practiced it since Weimar. At least we did not fall down on the icy road.

LeClaire was in seventh heaven. "Men, I tell you, next summer we will parade like this on the Red Square in Moscow, and then we will go home!"

Nobody wanted to destroy Lieutenant LeClaire's happiness. After a few more drinks inside the hut the party broke up.

. . .

CHAPTER 20

We did not stay too long in the Leningrad area. Our unit had to transfer to a town called Rshew, some miles further south. It was a difficult drive through ice and snow. We stayed in a little village close to the town.

I had to ask to see a physician because my stomach bothered me a lot, probably from all these depressing developments. I hitchhiked into Rshew and found the hospital. The doctor pumped my stomach and found signs of gastritis. "Just try milder food, like cream and lots of milk, nothing that can irritate your stomach."

He had to be kidding. Army food with milk and cream and eggs and white bread? Where did he live? In Switzerland?

When the doctor examined me he found some lice in my hair. He insisted on keeping me overnight and supplied a large turban dressing with Cuprex. The solution burned like fire, and I could not sleep.

In the bunk below and the one next to that two apparently older soldiers were talking. I could not help overhearing their conversation.

"Isn't it a shame, Rolf - do you see that soldier there, apparently blind? And the others who have lost a hand or part of a leg! They are maybe twenty years old, and they are shot up, or lost fingers or toes from that damned cold. What is their life going to be like? What good have they seen in their life so far? Nothing but rough duty and killing...."

"No, Juergen, they never had a normal life, and they are not going to have any from now on either. At least we had a few good years, had a job, didn't you? Did some drinking before we got married. They will never see that life like we did. You can say what you want, but this damned war is a sin against life."

"You said it. A sin against life, making them sacrifice their health, their future - everything for the fatherland. I wish I could do something against all that nonsense, but what?"

He apparently got his pipe ready, stuffed it and then lit it and puffed for a while. A wonderful tobacco aroma wafted up to me. Must be American or British tobacco, I thought.

"Where did you get that tobacco from, Klaus? That is a great aroma, man."

"Take some, please, roll yourself a cigarette. Just don't ask me where I got it from." The soldier laughed. Then he continued.

"How did we get into all this? Oh ja, seeing these wounded guys, the ones who lost so much. I have to tell you, we at least had some money. I had a good job with the brewery. We looked forward to Mardi Gras every year, and those were wild times. All that beer - you know what I mean: the girls..."

Their conversation drifted to Carnival festivities in Duesseldorf or Cologne and the girls they had met. After a while they must have forgotten completely that they were in this hospital, far away from Duesseldorf, in this cold and lonely Russian town.

My turban dressing caused too much burning pain. I was sure no lice could have survived, so I took the dressing off. I felt much better right away and must have gone to sleep after a short while.

I woke up early in the morning. A woman doctor was standing at the side of my bunk bed. She had fine features in her face, had blond hair and big blue eyes. She looked more Western European than Russian. Maybe she was from Latvia or Lithuania.

"Soldier, you knew that you were not allowed to take that dressing off," she spoke good German. "Anyway, let me check your hair."

She went through almost every strand of my hair and apparently she was satisfied. Then she stepped back and said, "You have beautiful eyes, soldier, do you know that?" She looked at me silently for a while.

"All right, you may go now. Good luck, Soldier."

I felt embarrassed. But then, wasn't she a little reminder of civilization, of a different life besides army and bad food and partisans and cold weather, a life I had almost forgotten. I took it as such, and almost started to think of Hamburg. But that would be stupid. I was not in Hamburg; I was in Rshew, in the northwestern part of Russia.

It would have been hard for anybody to tolerate what happened shortly thereafter when I was hitchhiking back to my unit.

I had gotten a ride on an army truck. We had to stop at a railroad crossing. It was brutally cold, and even sitting in the cab of the truck did not help much. The heater could not keep up with an icy wind from the East that penetrated everything.

A long train passed by. It rolled very slowly, jerking and screeching in the connectors and couplings. All were open cattle cars, and wagon after wagon was the same; the cars were crammed with Russian POW's. Nobody could have fallen down even if they wanted to. Some of the men had caps on, or coats, but many did not. They were just standing there, already half frozen to death, their faces expressionless. Most of them had ice in their hair or in mustaches and eyebrows. They did not even bother anymore to wipe it off. German soldiers with rifles and submachine guns trained on the prisoners rode in special cars. Their faces were stoic and grim.

All the prisoners would be dead in a day or so if the train would keep on running. The German border was two or three days away, maybe even longer if the train continued with that slow speed. Was this the way POW's were being treated? Frozen to death?

Finally the train passed. I was shaking. For the first time I was proud that I had gastritis or other symptoms from being affected by cruelties I had seen and by the criminal stupidity of the High Command. At least I was still capable of reacting; I still had some compassion for human life.

From now on I stopped writing home. I could not write about what I had seen in Rshew. Too many letters were censored. And why should I write about the pretty birch trees and the little huts, and that I was doing fine. It seemed to be so ridiculous.

After a few weeks my mother wrote to Lieutenant Hornberg and asked why I had not written and whether I was okay. I was called to see Hornberg, but he did not even ask why I did not write home. Maybe he could figure it out, maybe a few other men had done the same. I knew ,though, that I had added a few more minus points on his score card that had labeled me already a marked man.

"We have got the Cholm traffic. Here are the frequencies and the call letters. Osten, Heller, get ready right now!"

Sergeant Bass had come in from the cold outside. He brushed the snow off his coat and took his boots off.

Cholm was a little hamlet not too far away. It was occupied by German forces, but the Russians had surrounded it and kept attacking it every day. It was a strategically important place. We had to hold it.

The last few weeks had been boring. There was little traffic for us. Most communications went by phone.

But now it felt as if we were back in the "golden days" of the summer campaign. We were busy day and night to keep the connection open. Then one of the two remaining radio operators in Cholm was wounded and needed to be replaced. Hornberg asked for volunteers. I was in a desperate enough mood to volunteer. Maybe this way I can get out of this misery, I thought. Or I get it over with, with a little bit of glory.

But I was not accepted. Another man was sent by glider plane into the little city. These supply gliders were towed to the vicinity of Cholm and then released. They usually made an uneventful landing near the houses of Cholm. Some of the pilots did not make it, some of them wound up in Russian hands.

The glider crews joined the defenders of Cholm, since there was no way back. When I was reading the list of the pilots, I noticed that Heinz Voelker, a friend from the days of the Flying Hitler youth camp, was one of them.

Adolf Hitler had noticed the courageous fight of the Cholm soldiers and sent a telegram congratulating them on their perseverance, promising help as soon as possible. Easy for him, I thought as I was deciphering this message. He is sitting safely in his bunker in Rastenburg, East Prussia.

The following months brought nothing but continuous snow, ice cold winds and a lot of boredom. It was so easy to start worrying and feel depressed if you were not busy. I found some pocket books my mother had sent me. I read them and fought hard to keep my spirit up.

Mail came every so often. I received a letter from Nolle, who apparently was not far away from us. He wrote that he was "in the coldest part of Russia." That was around here, we knew that. Wouldn't it be something if I could meet with him somewhere here? No, technically this was impossible. There was no way that I could find out what unit he belonged to, and where this unit might be.

Wolf sent a letter also, and I did not like what he wrote. Sure, I felt sorry that he still had medical problems and that he had fallen further behind in his schedule. But then he said that he had seen Signe a couple of times, when he was on sick-leave in Hamburg. She was the same, cheered him up a lot and they had dinner at his house. He had to go back to Bremerhaven after a few days.

I still believed in our promise not to get involved until the war was over, but it now was a little bit harder. Hadn't she said that clearly? Despite the promises she had made, it was like a hot iron going through my body. What if they maybe "broke down" and had gone all the way....I calmed myself down with a lot of effort. I wished he were far away like me, maybe in Africa or some other place.

Then I remembered what Mrs. Hammer once had said: "There is no girl in the world worth killing yourself for."

No, but I had become very restless, I could not deny that.

Finally April arrived and we thought it might get a little warmer. But all fields were still covered with heavy layers of snow. And we knew that snow would be on the ground usually until May.

There was much talk about what the coming summer would bring. A new, big offensive? Where? Overall most of us soldiers had become pretty cynical, and the morale was affected deeply by the disastrous winter.

The latest word then was that we would not be a part of the coming offensive. We had the impression that the generals themselves were not sure what the best strategy would be. Then suddenly the news came, that we would be sent to the center of the Russian front and would be transported to Roslawl.

Summer did arrive and now an unexpected bonus came our way; we would be able to get leave, one man of each troop at a time. At the end of July finally it was my turn.

But I found out that I really wasn't looking forward to it as much as I thought I would. None of my friends would be there. The food was reportedly so scarce at home that I was glad that they gave us food stamps to take home. I knew that Vinci still was around. But now he was helping my mother a lot with errands and repairs of the house and the endless paperwork which dealt with one restriction after another, one demand after another, even if you were not a party member.

I also was not so sure about meeting Signe. I wanted to be very careful, but also I wanted to know what was going on. I knew I could take the truth, even if it was a bitter pill.

I took the long train ride through northern Russia, Estonia, Latvia and Lithuania into Poland and East Prussia, and then to Berlin and Hamburg.

The trip took four days. First we saw a lot of destruction that was caused by the partisans, like blown-up bridges, destroyed railroad tracks, abandoned railroad cars or engines that had been pushed off the tracks; some of them were already rusting.

All trees, bushes and shrubbery to each side of the railroad tracks had been cut down for a thousand feet as a safety zone, so the partisans would have no place to hide. The first car of each train was a flatbed car filled with sand. It would take the first blow if mines had been planted. The next car had machine guns and anti-aircraft cannons.

At every bridge the train slowed down almost to a halt. There had been so much damage to the bridges, and most of them were repaired only tentatively.

As we came to Germany, however, everything looked much more normal. Berlin itself looked normal, except that there was very little automobile traffic. Thousands of people were walking on the streets or riding in streetcars and buses, not being able to drive: practically no gasoline was available for the average citizen.

I was back in Germany.

. . .

CHAPTER 21

The trip from Berlin to Hamburg was uneventful. A gnawing feeling, though, became stronger and stronger; what if my mother or grandmother had been killed in the meantime or our house had been destroyed.

As I walked the last few hundred yards to our house I saw the unbelievable destruction, the heaps of rubble, the smashed trees. We were in line with an important oil refinery, and many attempts had been made to hit this complex, Bombs hads missed it and ravaged our neighborhood.

By now my heart was racing. Then I saw it; our house was standing up all right. There was a long crack from the basement to the roof, but apparently not causing any structural problems. Thank God.

I found my mother and grandmother to be in fairly good shape, but over-tired from all the trips to the air raid shelter which was half a mile away. Since the bombs had struck so close to our house, they had decided to make that trip every time the air raid sirens blared away. They always carried their valuables with them.

My mother did everything to make it easy on me. She was glad that I had brought some food stamps and that she did not have to worry about feeding me. We avoided serious discussions about any problem. I thought it was better to let things go and not to bother each other with our concerns. Maybe it was.

The usually dynamic and even lively city of Hamburg was dead. No nightlife, nothing in the stores to go shopping for, buses and streetcars were running only irregularly. No taxis.

Daily or twice daily air raid alarms made you hesitate to go anywhere. None of my friends was home.

I tried Signe a few times. Nobody answered the phone. When I visited Wolf's parents, they were very happy to see me and talk with me. But I also noticed that they were somewhat uneasy; something bothered them, but they did not say anything. I learned that Wolf still had trouble with his gallbladder ,that his progress had been slowed down a lot. They hoped he would get on a ship in a month, though.

There was not much to do in Hamburg. I went to see Klaus Rieder's father who was an important man in the clothing industry. Maybe he could tell me a little more, give me some information about the war situation. He was very friendly, and told me the somewhat tragic and also funny story his son had told him. He had a girlfriend in Berlin and tried to call her. After waiting on army telephone lines for four hours he finally got through to her house. By then it was evening. Her mother answered the phone, and when he asked whether her daughter was home, she said, "Yes, she is, but she does not take any calls after nine P.M."

Klaus was in Sevastopol, in Southern Russia, 1200 miles away.

I found enough courage to ask Mr. Rieder what he thought of the war. I knew it was a pretty aggressive question, but I wanted to know what was going on. Nobody I felt gave you a truthful answer. Maybe he would.

Mr. Rieder hesitated a moment, then cleared his throat a few times. "Dietz,...I believe we will win the war. It might take us longer, yes, but ultimately we will win." I don't know, but I had noticed that he had hesitated, that his answer was not free and spontaneous. He definitely had his own thoughts about everything, and I believe my question had bothered him. I felt that this gentleman was not so sure about the war at all.

I appreciated his answer, and maybe I should not have asked. But then I was a soldier, my life was at stake, I wanted to know what our chances were.

The wording of the propaganda machine had changed. After years of talking about nothing but victory, they now changed this to "final" victory. That was quite a different attitude.

I tried Signe again. No answer.

When my time was almost up I really did not mind going back to Russia. At least I had the feeling that I was doing something there, instead of being home and hearing nothing but complaints about the scarcity of food, about the daily and nightly air raids, and noticing nothing but fear when mail came; somebody else might have been killed in action. Like Hagerman, who had been killed in Norway, Kasten, who was missing near

Leningrad, apparently killed in his fighter plane, and Hansen, who was killed in the fighting around Kiew. They were all schoolfriends or guys I knew from the Hitler Youth.

Also, what happened to Signe? Did she go to Sweden after all? The Rohrbach's had not even mentioned her. Something was not right.

The next day Wolf Rohrbach called. He just had left the hospital after a final check. He felt fine and expected to be on active duty in a few weeks. Then he said, clearly haltingly, "You know, Signe is here. Did my parents tell you?"

It was as if lightning had struck me. Signe,-- visiting Wolf? I could not say anything for a while.

"Dietz, are you there? She came to me,--please understand ! It just happened,--please dont't get mad,--it is a natural thing, you know,Dietz, we both are mature enough, please settle down-- we made plans---"

"What kind of pl--plans?" I stuttered.

"Dietz! We made plans about going to college, where and what we were going to study. I am thinking of business school, and she might want to go into interior decorating."

"Well- I don't know--I thought we had an agreement not to --- well, it is done now. Good bye."

I slammed the receiver down.

I was the loser in our "love" triangle. For her to travel to Bremerhaven -. Well, Dietz, take it easy. Remember what Mrs. Hammer said about girls and suicide?--- There would be other girls. Get over this now and look around later.

.

CHAPTER 22

I was standing in the train gangway, still numb from what Wolf had told me , halfway listening to the familiar clickety-clack of the wheels. A little voice appeared somewhere in my mind. "Okay, Dietz, you were suspicious, and you were right.Forget about it,other people had similar problems - and they stayed calm. Don't feel sorry for yourself."

I knew I had to get over this, as soon as possible.

All right, but I can't help being...upset.

. . .

The train arrived in Berlin in the afternoon. I was to change again at the Anhalter Bahnhof. But there were officers from the Field Gendarmery telling us that no train to the Eastern Front would run for a few days since a bridge across the Oder River had been blown up. We were given some different tickets and a note confirming the delay. I sat down in the cafeteria, which was not far away from the tracks.

Next to my table there were a few air force helper girls in their blue uniforms. They were chatting lively and had a good time. I looked closer. There was Ulla! The girl I had met in Freiburg, when we visited Pat and his friend Rudi!

She also must have recognized me. She came over to my table, a cup of coffee in her hand. "Hi, Dietz,...I don't believe it! What are you doing here?"

"Hi, Ulla, it is wonderful to see you!" She sat down with me. She told me that she was now an air force helper, a radio operator, attending a course in coding, and that she stayed in an apartment that Rudi's sister let her have while she was out of town. She was so lucky that she did not have to stay in barracks.

Ulla then went back and brought her tray over. The girls looked but kept on chatting.

"Ulla, I thought you were studying medicine in Freiburg?"

"Yes, I was, but then wounded soldiers took our places. We have to wait for now. But you - you look really good! You must have grown an inch or two. Are you coming or going?"

"I am going, going back to Russia. Our train, though, has been delayed, and I am not in any hurry. Let's go somewhere, where we can talk better. Are you tied up?"

"No, we are done for the day. Why don't we go to my apartment, it is not far from here. I want to hear all about you and your brother. I have not been in Freiburg for a long time."

I was surprised to notice the feeling of some immediate contact with her. When we came to the apartment I was amazed to see the elegance, the fine furniture and some good copies of paintings on the walls, one of them being my one of my favorite paintings at that time, a Caspar David Friedrich landscape. I felt as if I almost was at home, although everything was much more expensive than in our house.

First I was somewhat apprehensive, having not had any experience with meeting a girl in her apartment. But I relaxed soon. Ulla made real coffee; not the "Ersatz coffee" I had grown used to. She then found enough food to make a little dinner.

Ulla told me that she was in the airforce signal corps and had been trained as a radio operator. We talked about the equipment we were using and about the Enigma machine with which she was very familiar. We both wished we had less antique radio equipment, that we had the British Morse key. Ours was so clumsy. Then we talked about unusual messages we had transmitted at one time or another.

Ulla said that she might be transferred to the big air raid warning center near Hamburg, but for the time this was just a possibility.

I now felt relaxed, but also full of anticipation. It was so good to be with this girl, who had dark, flowing hair, beautiful big eyes and soft and tender looking skin.

Ulla found a bottle of wine, and while we were drinking slowly, she put some records on. First it was Zarah Leander with her dark, sultry voice, singing "Der Wind hat mir ein Lied erzaehlt." Then I found my favorite

German song, "Bei Dir war es immer so schoen," a haunting melody about loving and then having to leave. Yes, could it not be like that with the two of us?

Everything developed then in a very natural way while the sun was setting over the rooftops. Both of us were in a dreamy mood, maybe not thinking that much about each other, but forlorn in memories of the prewar days. We also were acutely aware of the fact that we had been caught in deadly events that could bring our end any day. Why not live our life, now? We were only young once.

Ulla let her head rest on my shoulder. Then I knew that she was as ready as I was.

"Dietz, why don't you stay with me tonight. Will you?"

"Ulla, I would love to very much."

It was now dark. We undressed, showered and went to bed. I began to kiss her gently all over. She responded to my soft stroking.

We kissed for a long time. Then I heard her murmuring, "It is okay - it is safe."

Our bodies became entwined. We both forgot about thinking and worrying. She was so natural and gratifying in her response. I felt lucky to be together with this girl, even if it would be just for a short time. It was much better than all those stories I had heard about the girls in France from Osten or Schmitty, true or not. Forget about Signe.

"Bei Dir war es immer so schoen." I had to hear that song again. I got up and cranked the record player, and reset the needle. Then I went back to bed and held Ulla again. We were like two children seeking and finding refuge from all the grim things that were going on around us. I felt complete peace and satisfaction as I held her and then watched her while she slept.

The warm summer wind played with the camouflage curtains on the open windows. It brought warm air up from the pavement of the street below, and the voices of people talking down there. The record needle kept on clicking after the song ended, then it stopped.

I must have gone to sleep too.

Both of us woke up when the air raid sirens started to wail. I trusted my instinct and experience and was not going to go to the shelter unless there was acute danger.

For a while we listened to the rumbling of anti-aircraft fire in the distance. Gradually it subsided. Maybe it just was a reconnaissance plane.

We were almost asleep when the all-clear signal sounded. My last thoughts were how great it was to be here with this beautiful girl, as I was looking at her in the dim shine of the night-light.

Maybe one of these days everything would be all right after all, and I could lead a life where a girl like her would be a part of it. Damned stupid war.

I woke up at about 8 a.m. Ulla was gone. I was not at all eager to get up.

What a fantastic night it had been, besides the loving. Both of us woke up at about two o'clock and started to talk about the wrongs of this war, the worries, the uselessness of all this dying and sacrificing. This was the first time I could talk with a civilian, a woman, not having to worry about what I said. Ulla felt very much the same, and to my surprise then hinted that my brother Pat, Rudi and few other friends were involved in some underground activities. She did not say much, and I don't blame her. But the fact that she mentioned my brother was important enough. I started to figure out a way that I could ask him about it. No, not by mail. Too much of it was censured.

I stretched out again and enjoyed the bed for a few more minutes. How long had it been that I had slept in a bed, besides at home ? Yes, in Arcachon in France, and with Georg Osten! I had to smile.

Well, I did not have to go to the station until tomorrow. Ulla had left a note saying that she would be back by six p.m. I went downtown to see a few places I had wanted to see for quite some time. Back to the eastern front tomorrow.

. . .

CHAPTER 23

The two days with Ulla helped me after the bitter experience with Wolf and Signe. I knew I could forget Signe now.

When I came back to my unit I could already smell the coming fall up here in the north. Some leaves had started to change colors.

We were now located on the banks of a muddy, brownish river. We lived in one of the typical huts or blockhouses. Occasionally Russian artillery sent some heavy shells across the river. Fortunately the rounds fell short. At night Russian planes flew overhead making endless circles. Their engines sounded so tinny that we soldiers immediately called them "sewing machines". But they kept on cruising for hours like relentless mosquitoes and kept everybody awake. Occasionally they dropped bombs. They fell far away from our village. One plane, though, crashed. The soldiers at the crash scene found a woman pilot in it.

Every soldier who had gone through the last winter in Russia was given a special medal, a red band with black and white stripes in the center. These medals immediately received a number of unflattering nicknames, like "Frozen Meat Medal", or "Rollbahn Medal", referring to the murderously cold winter, when German forces in an immense "red" country were trying to hold on to their positions, having only a "rollbahn" as a connecting life line to their "Hinterland".

Hitler gave a speech and we all stood around the loudspeakers, hoping against hope that he would have some good news. No, it was all rhetoric and no substance. Propaganda kept on hammering into us that a great victory was near. We knew better. Even the most ardent Nazis in our unit had become Doubting Thomases and remained suspiciously quiet. Where were the "secret" weapons he had promised? Even Heinrich von Ellsleben showed no open enthusiasm, but was very quiet and sullen. He did not tell anybody that victory was close. That was the first time.

. . .

I tried to make plans, just in case I would somehow survive the war. I wanted to have some goal. Okay, I was a good and experienced radio operator, but that was by far not enough. I thought more and more about studying medicine. But how? My mother never had promised that she would be able to send me to college. The chances of getting a loan were poor in those years in Germany. Enlist as a medical student with the armed forces? No, I could not take that. It would be like army life all over.

I could not expect any help from my father.... That's when I became a gambler. Enroll at a University anyhow, just to get out from Russia. I had done my share here. After two years of service you could get a discharge if you studied medicine. At least try! Life here is useless. Maybe you can find some way of financing once you get into medical school. Maybe my grandmother could give me a loan. My thoughts went back and forth. Then I just applied for admission at the Medical School where Pat was now finishing up.

The restlessness apparently was common, other guys like Karl Weber were trying to make plans too. It was not very busy, again most of the traffic went by phone.

Dieter Siebert from troop three came over one day. He had just returned from his leave and he really was beaming; "Guys, I got married when I was home. You know, in this mess it is good to have somebody who loves you and belongs to you. We don't have any great amount of money, but I can have a job as a painter when I come back. We are not so much materially inclined. We might even have a baby, an heir. That would be great!" He was genuinely happy, I thought, until one of the men from our troop said - I believe it was Kretzschmar - "Yes, and those who are married are not being assigned to dangerous missions. They will not be transferred to the infantry."

That opened my eyes. Maybe his decision to marry was then pretty pragmatic, I thought. Dietz, I hope you don't fool yourself.

. . .

Georg Osten had his little problems too. He had met this beautiful girl in Duesseldorf, and they were thinking of marrying. But now she wrote him that she was not so sure about it all and wanted to see him a few more times before deciding.

Finally Schmitty - that is Karl Schmitt, who graciously had consented to us calling him "Schmitty" - killed the conversation with a somewhat devious grin. "You know that I am married, but I had a great time in France." Again he pulled out the stack of pictures of the prostitutes. We knew them so well by now, actually, we knew the name of each of them; Nicole, Sarah and Coco.

I had not seen Richie Gattorna for a long time. He had been made to work in the repair shop for trucks and cars. Their workshop usually was a few miles back.

Richie had become friends with Georg Osten. The three of us one night took some sweet, dark wine, which had been issued to the troops, and got together in a hut close to ours. We all had much to talk about after our leaves. Georg Osten was enthralled with this girl in Duesseldorf, and I was telling them about my meeting with Ulla, leaving Signe's story out completely. But as usual, Richie would trump us with his experiences, true or imaginary, I still didn't know. He had met Juanita Bauer, the girl who had been involved with Wolf Rohrbach at one time. "She knows you, Dietz."

It was dark, and we had a large kettle, poured the wine into it, and placed what should have been a metal tongue across it. We had found some metal, which would do just as well. Richie had brought a large lump of sugar. We poured vodka on it and lit it. It burned with a blue flame, and the melting sugar dropped into the wine, making it even sweeter - and stronger. It was all pretty exciting. We helped sample the brew until we found it to be right, and sampling was a repeated and important part of the procedure, until all of us felt well. Richie was at his best. "Dietz, that Juanita Bauer...I tell you, she is quite a girl. She could not wait, and we did it right there on the living room couch. There was a very expensive vase standing right next to it. It started to rattle and then sway as we humped along. It nearly fell. I had to tear myself away from the girl and grab the vase just in time. But what a girl, I tell you..."

"Yes, Juanita Bauer, I remember her well. She was known to be a pretty hot item."

I remembered her dancing with Wolf, almost completely fused to his body. Oh, I did not need this memory, because it immediately brought up Signe's picture.

Forget about those two, man! Be glad it is over!

I pulled myself together and made myself think of Ulla, had a good time and wound up with the expected headache.

. . .

Two days later Richie called. He almost was crying. "I got a telegram, I don't know how it got through. But my father was killed and my mother was seriously injured in an air raid. She might lose her left leg. I talked with Hornberg, and he will let me go home for a few days. Oh my God, this war is horrible. What shall I do?"

What could I say? I just stammered some words of consolation, that I was so sorry...but what can you really do?

"Richie - let me see you, let's talk. Maybe I can help. When are you leaving?"

"I will get out tomorrow."

"I will be over in a few minutes. I am not on call until tonight."

I met him shortly after. We sat down in the cab of a radio truck. I let him cry. Maybe that would do him some good.

"Dietz, I might have put on a cheerful face all these months. But I am so fed up with the war, the nonsense, the killing - for what? I need to get somewhere where I am needed, to have some counterweight against all the cruelty. I don't mind, but I think I will volunteer for the pioneers, do something positive instead of repairing all the beat-up trucks, answer some challenges to divert my mind. I don't know. I don't like to kill...."

We talked for quite a while until I had to go back to my troup. He left the next day for Hamburg.

I was sitting on the main receiver, listening for any calls for us. We always had a second receiver on in order to take emergency messages on a different frequency. I must admit that everyone of us liked to switch to BBC London in order to get some more acurate news. The station came clear through even here in Northern Russia. The great story according to BBC London now was that Russia had found a big Ally, "General Winter." And how true it was. The whole German Army was hopelessly bogged down in ice and snow, and they would be lucky to survive this winter.

No, Heinrich would not let himself down to share this bad habit. Whoever was on with him - like on a busy day - was condemned to listen to the Emergency frequency. Sergeant Bass naturally would not think of anything like that either, until I heard the familiar BBC sign coming out of his receiver one night, when I had to go to the bathroom. The sergeant apparently very busy writing a letter had not noticed me. Welcome to the club.

A few days later I made one mistake when I asked Osten to relieve me for a moment; I did not turn BBC off. And sure, Heinrich noticed it and reported it gleefully to Sergeant Bass. Both of them seemed to be childishly happy to have caught me.

It then was the usual procedure; to report to Lieutenant Hornberg and Captain Schultz. I was astonished to notice that I was pretty fatalistic about it. Lieutenant Hornberg gave a standard speech and declared that now I was a marked man and should be very careful. Hornberg then sentenced me to six weeks hard labor; I had to get up at 4 AM and help the cook with his chores, walking two miles through heavy snow. The cook was a friend of Heinrich's and definitely did not make it easy on me. I wondered why I did not seem to mind at all.

When I came back to the troup I immediately was placed on the main receiver. Sergeant Bass and Georg Osten were looking on, while Schmitty sat in the background, waiting for something to happen.

Heinrich turned around to me in the sweetest way, smiling with the most generous smile I ever had seen, and asked me "My dear friend, may I set the dial on BBC London ?"

That was it. My fist shot forward and I still can feel the softness of his skin and the hardness of his jaw. It was a solid hit.

He started to bleed a little, tore his handkerchief out and held it tight against his mouth. He did look at me very strangely, full of reproach, but did not do anything like fighting back. Now I knew he was a coward.

I even heard Sergeant Bass laugh his strange laugh. Georg Osten said calmly; "You needed that, Heinrich." And Schmitty in the background laughed and laughed and cried "Bravo, Dietz!"

Heinrich got up silently. Still holding his handkerchief to his mouth, he put on his coat and uniform cap and left the hut.

I realized that it was about time that I should ask for a transfer to another unit. I was a marked man since the BBC affair, and for not having written to my mother. I was from Hamburg and almost everybody else was from Frankfurt or from Thuringia. They stuck together. They would do anything to prevent that one of them would have to go to the infantry.

And I was the youngest man. There was much talk about the younger ones to be shipped to the infantry. I guessed that I would be sent with the first group.

At that time I conceived for the first time a brutally dangerous and crazy plan. Why not volunteer as an officer's candidate for the infantry? It would mean weeks and weeks in a training unit in Germany, and I possibly could be trained as a communication officer, teaching Morse code, etc. The thought of shooting people still was completely unacceptable for me. Sure, that was a dangerous plan, but to be transferred to the infantry without proper training was far worse.

There was another reason for me to consider transfer: All this time it seemed to me a big secret: how could those infantry guys live in constant danger, what kept them going? Were they different human beings or did they have as special philosophy which kept them going?

I had to find out. I had developed a great understanding for them. I knew that if I did not find out it always would bother me.

I had started to kick this idea in my head back and forth. Why not? This unit here was stagnant. I wanted to go forward, somewhere. Like those Cabballeros in my song about the River of Gold; "We will find you, and your treasures! Amigos, let's go!" No, more important to me was to find their secret. to have something to tell which would at least equal my mothers lover's stories, which had made me sick as he told them again and again.

Dietz, dare it: Go! Go, man ,now!

. . .

Heinrich von Ellsleben started to talk about going to the tank units. He was bored here and wanted some action. His father had written and asked him how many Russians he had killed so far.

Everybody seemed to be restless. The probability of spending another winter in this God-forlorn land, where there was nothing to enjoy and nothing to do - the ever-increasing activities of partisans, and for some the doubts about the whole campaign had killed the fighting spirit of most of the soldiers.

My hopes of going to medical school were dashed when the University notified me that I needed three more months in the service before I could be considered for enrollment.

Could I not wait? No, I knew something was up. But what? I had the feeling that I should not wait. I went back to the idea of volunteering for the infantry. I had not made up my mind when I received a number of letters from home, from Mr. and Mrs. Rohrbach and from Signe. Wolf's boat was lost in the battle of the Atlantic.

That hit me really hard.

Mr. Rohrbach wrote that they had lost contact with Captain Unger's submarine. All boats of his wolfpack had tried again and again. After a week it was declared a total loss. Mrs. Rohrback's words were particularly saddening, showing the inability to cope with it all, showing her bottomless grief.

Signe's letter was very much the same. I tried to read it three times. I felt sorry for her. But it was different than it would have been half a year ago. It was as if a fog was in front of my mind when I thought of her.

Why should Wolf die, and I, with my miserable outlook on this war should survive? Forget the thoughts of jealousy I had entertained. They seemed to be so petty now.

I was confused and desperate. I knew I would go crazy if I did not do something, find a way of life where I would not wonder and think about it day and night.

I volunteered for officer's training in the infantry.

. . .

CHAPTER 24

I was accepted by an infantry unit within a few days and I actually was on my way faster than I expected. I had said good-bye to my troup. Most of them shook their head and thought that I was crazy. Karl Weber was on an assignment, and I could not talk with him. Roland was not at his troup either. Heinrich von Ellsleben acknowledged my departure with a fiendish grin, and he did not say one word.

Georg Osten walked me to the train station. I tried to explain to him why I had volunteered. He could not understand my action, but he was very friendly and sympathetic.

It was a chilly day in October when I left. Some snow was on the ground. I had to meet a train at a lonely pick-up station. It brought me further east, then discharged me at another lonely stop. Nobody was there to meet me. I happened to know the logo of the infantry division and started to walk following their signs.

Some artillery was active, banging erratic shots here and there. Occasionally a machine gun rattled away. Otherwise it was quiet. I wondered why I was not afraid. I probably was too desperate to feel any fear. I was following my own decision though, and I knew I could blame only myself for what was going to happen.

I saw a tree stump at the side of the road and sat down. This was a good occasion to find out what the transfer letter said that Hornberg had sent along. I carefully opened it. It was easy to do since it was not fully sealed.

"Pfc. Dietz Heller has made good progress as a soldier. He should be able to become a fine officer, dedicated to his duties...etc."

I was somewhat surprised. He did not mention that I had been punished for listening to a foreign radio station. He probably was glad to get rid of me. No, I think he did not care one way or the other.

. . .

I found the infantry unit without too much difficulty and then met Lieutenant Schwarzenberg and a few other officers.

Schwarzenberg told me that I would be treated like any common soldier so I would learn how they felt and how they lived. This was the new spirit in the army, he said, and they would not tolerate anything that could lead to development of the old class system: officers against common men. I had to agree that this was progressive thinking, whether the Nazis had introduced it or not. He also told me that they were going to watch me closely. He promised to send me to officer's school in about eight weeks if I did well. He then said:" Corporal Konjetzxny will be your superior. You do what he tells you to do."

I met Stanislaus and Fritz, two soldiers from Upper Silesia. I was to live with them in a very small bunker. It was not even a bunker; it was a hole in the ground about three times the size of a foxhole. You really had to twist yourself to enter it through a very narrow entrance. It was covered with logs and a layer of dirt on top. A small hole at the foot end was used as a fireplace and it had a straight upward outlet, acting as a chimney. You had to keep the fire going; otherwise the cold air would rush in immediately.

At night we laid ourselves down there, our feet toward the fireplace. There was not one inch to spare. Fritz and Stanislaus were simple and tough guys. Their life would be the one of a coal miner. They told me that years ago there was a great disaster, when an explosion killed several hundred miners. The administration wanted to close the mine for good. But the miners protested. It was the only job they could get there, and they said they rather would want to die a fast death in the mines than slowly die of starvation. The mine stayed open.

They talked usually very fast with a heavy Silesian accent. It was hard for me to say much, but they were friendly and gradually I could make better contact with them.

Our life consisted of weapon drills, shooting practice and guard duty. The front was quiet, but Fritz told me that they had taken prisoners recently from Russian units unknown to them so far. Everybody took that as a sign that the Russians were preparing for an offensive.

But we had no water to wash with, unless you melted snow. We used some of our coffee rations to brush our teeth. There was no latrine; you took a spade and went, and when the ground was frozen, you just went. We lived day and night in our winter uniforms with no chance to change even our underwear.

Occasionally a corporal or sergeant came and took me to show me new weapons like the machine gun that could shoot eight hundred rounds per minute. At one time a sergeant took me to a group of very high fir trees near the front line. We had to be very careful.

"See that man up there, Heller?"

"No, I can't see anything, Sergeant."

"Man, look up there in that fir tree! That is one of our soldiers, hiding near the top, observing the whole valley."

"Oh, now I see it, and the phone line. Yes, sir."

"He stays there all day long, comes down at night. Great job, and has he ever helped us when the Russians attacked."

That man could not move all day long. How he could stand this murderous cold nobody knew.

. . .

I developed an abscess on my left heel. There had been no chance to keep our feet clean or even change socks. I went to the battalion physician and had it lanced. I got some Sulfa tablets, but they did not help. I went back to my bunker without a chance to really clear up the abscess.

I did not hear anything from Lieutenant Schwarzenberg for a good while. Then he called me to his bunker.

"At ease, Heller. I have decided to send you on a scouting patrol, maybe tonight or tomorrow night, whenever the moon is strong enough. I want you to make the rounds of our three forward posts, find them, check them and go on. If you do that all right, we will send you to Germany. You will have to do this all by yourself. I can not risk a bunch of guys so you get your Iron Cross. It will be a chance for you to show us what you have got inside of yourself.

Sergeant Obermuth will give you a map of the minefields, the Russians and ours. Study it and learn it by heart. You cannot take it with you."

We will let you know when you will do it. Dismissed."

I went to Sergeant Obermuth's bunker and got the map of the minefields. Obermuth shook his head. "What is he doing? Send you out there, all by yourself? Nobody goes out there without at least two other soldiers."

I started to read the instructions and study the map. I had found a small candle to give me some light. Stanislaus and Fritz came into our bunker. I told them about the planned patrol.

"Man, he must be crazy!" said Stanislaus. "Nobody goes out there ever alone! Especially not a new man!" And Fritz added, "Stan, let us tell Konjetzny about this!"

"Why Konjetzny?" I asked.

"Corporal Konjetzny is the watchdog committee. It was set up some time ago when Schwarzenberg misdirected the grenade throwers and they killed three of our men. The parents of these men and many other people wrote in and demanded an explanation. And then this committee was set up to check on certain practices of the officers. Now Konjetzny has something to say whenever unnecessary risks were taken. When a problem like this comes up Konjetzny is right there. We think it is a great idea - we feel a little more protected."

"No thanks - let it go" I said. "I think I can do it. It will make a bad impression if I go over there now and argue with him."

"You are crazy," said Stanislaus, "but go ahead if you really have to. I would not. I would talk to Konjetzny."

"Yes, Stan, but he is an officer's candidate," Fritz interjected. "He cannot really refuse. They might send him to officer's school right afterwards."

But Stan was not through yet. "I bet he would not have dared to send anybody from Waldenburg or Kosel out on a mission like this. He is just trying to get rid of..."

He never finished the sentence. He turned abruptly to the far wall and did not say another word.

Well, Lieutenant Schwarzenberg, I thought, I won't do you this favor. I am not going to get myself killed. Even if you prefer officer's candidates from Silesia or Upper Silesia.

The following night I was called again to Schwarzenberg's bunker. I received final instructions and the password, and then I took off.

A fine haze hung over the wooded area, but the moon was out and fairly bright. The ground haze created a strange impression as if I was walking through an immense hall; a little man trying to find his way in this vast snowy empire. I heard some rifle shots here and there, but the artillery was not active. Behind the Russian lines I heard some clanking of heavy equipment, maybe tanks. In the distance a train was rumbling along. How could that be? A train? That close to the front?

My heel started to burn like fire. I felt some moisture in my socks; the abscess had recurred and opened up again.

The first leg of my trip had to be aimed straight east towards the Russian lines. Initially I could make out something like a path through the underbrush. The ground, though, was covered with heavy snow, and the trees showed hoarfrost. Dense smoke hung low in the trees, having drifted this way from the German bunkers. The acrid smell of burnt wood was everywhere.

I stomped through the snow. The going was very cumbersome. After a while I saw a group of high fir trees, the first reference point. I had to turn to the right, otherwise I would be in the Russian minefields. My path led me to an open plain, and here the snow was even deeper.

I looked and looked. Fortunately I had the feeling that I was going in the right direction. Finally, after about half an hour, I suddenly saw a human figure ahead, and a rifle was pointed at me. I carefully spoke, almost hissed the password and received the right answer from the soldier who was standing guard at the first outpost. Both of us relaxed, exchanged a few words, and then I went inside the bunker and reported there. I gulped down a cup of hot coffee and then set forth again.

Probably God or some friendly spirit kept me from straying into the minefields as I now searched for the next outpost. Walking had become very exhausting, and my heel hurt like hell. Keep on going, man.

Where in hell was the second bunker?

Suddenly three white flares shot up over the Russian lines. I froze, did not move a bit until the flares died down. I was scared, but still did not run.

I heard some voices over there on the Russian side. Then they broke out into a song. A few lights appeared flickering erratically. Man, they had a party, they were drunk! Then a loud voice barked at them, and it suddenly became quiet.

I found the second bunker, and it was a little different. The guard almost shot me. He claimed that he had not been notified about me making the rounds. The sergeant in the second bunker immediately called company quarters, trying to find out what was going on and why they were not notified. He then called the third bunker and told them about me coming.

From now on the trip was anticlimactic, except that at one time a string of machine gun bullets whipped the snow up on my left. Had they seen me? I stopped dead in my tracks for a few minutes.

Then I went on, found the third bunker and checked in. Next I had to make a right turn. According to my memory there were no other minefields, and I thought I could proceed faster. Well, my left foot did not allow me to do that. The pain had become severe, and the whole leg felt like lead.

The moon was hiding now behind a heavy haze and orientation became somewhat difficult. After a while I noticed smoke in the air. I knew I was approaching the German lines. Finally I came to Schwarzenberg's bunker and entered it.

"Pfc. Heller reporting back..."

"Man, shake that snow off, will you?" That's about all he said, but he mumbled something that sounded like approval. Then he dismissed me.

Shortly thereafter I slipped into our three-man bunker and more or less collapsed next to Fritz and Stanislaus, who were snoring. As dead tired as I was and as the numbness of exhaustion seemed to be taking over, I knew that I had pretty much reached my goal, that is to experience the reality of war. For me it was now the knowledge that the superiors could do with you what they wanted. Nobody was there to check on them - well, maybe the watchdog committee.

Somehow I felt free now. And for the first time I now felt almost equal to Wolf Rohrbach.

Stanislaus and Fritz had made a good fire. I added a few pieces of firewood. Then the numbness of utter exhaustion took over, and I fell asleep.

. . .

There was quite some talk about my night patrol. Several soldiers came up to me, saying "How could he order you to go out there, at night, alone?" They certainly were critical of Lieutenant Schwarzenberg. I had the feeling that some of them had started to accept me.

My heel was getting worse. Now there was frank pus in my sock. This could not go on. I went again to the battalion first aid station. This time they kept me overnight, but it still was draining the next day. The medic kept me there to be seen by the physician. Again they loaded me up with Sulfonamides.

I felt feverish and weak and sank down on a cot in the first aid bunker, half in a daze.

The next morning the long expected attack by the Russians started. An uninterrupted artillery barrage hit the German lines. Rocket salvos followed again and again. Some artillery shells hit close by and made the bunker sway. At times it seemed to take a leap. Dirt was pouring from the ceiling, and the air pressure changes blew out the candles every few minutes. This then was the infamous "Trommelfeuer". I thought of the hated Vinci, who so many times had said that Trommelfeuer was like a baptism of battle, and everybody had to go through it at least once. It would separate the boys from the men and so on . . .

The German artillery answered and kept on pounding the Russians. Suddenly the Russian artillery stopped and then started to strike points far in the rear.

"They are coming now," one of the soldiers in our bunker said very casually. We could hear machine gun fire, hand grenades and rifle fire. Hand-to-hand combat must have ensued.

It all simmered down after an hour or two. The Russians had been repelled. Everybody felt relief. Only a few casualties came to our first aid bunker.

. . .

CHAPTER 25

After a few days I was discharged and found a ride on a horse-drawn sled back to the company. They had moved a few miles south. Now we were in the actual front line. I was assigned to Corporal Konjetzny's troup. "Ivan", as we called the Russians, was about a thousand feet away. We lived in larger bunkers. Our job was to stand sentry in little foxholes. It was so cold that nobody was allowed to be out there for more than one hour. After two hours of rest we had to go out again. This went on day and night. The bunkers only could be heated at night, and then only if the moon was not out. The smoke would give our position away, and we knew how accurate the Russian grenade fire could be.

I talked for a while with Corporal Joseph Konjetzny. He was a tall man with dark hair and very big hands. He was a powerful man, having worked as a miner for years. He had the Iron Cross first class and the infantry combat badge. The men clearly respected him.

The food was of poor quality and poor quantity. By the time the so-called warm food arrived it was cold, and in daytime we could not heat it up. Bread was frozen with ice crystals in it. We ate it anyway because we were so hungry. Everybody started to have diarrhea and stomach cramps. Then you had to go to the latrine in this bitter cold, sometimes sitting there for long minutes because of diarrhea. The excrements froze solidly like stalagmites, while a bright, brutally cold moon looked on.

No officer came around. Mail call was once a week. I received a nice long letter from Ulla. I could read between the lines that she now was in Hamburg at an air defense center. I wrote back to her, being very careful not to mention our circumstances. It would not do any good.

We had no chance to delouse ourselves because it was too cold to take our uniforms off. The anti-louse powder they gave us was completely ineffective and had a sickening smell to it.

Why did Schwarzenberg not communicate with me?

This life was hell, absolute hell. Nobody could imagine anything worse than this. I grimly decided that I never would want to forget this if I should survive. All this for those power-hungry leaders, and those generals who only could think of their Knight's Crosses.

I stumbled back into the bunker, my legs being almost stiffly frozen. I had just finished another tour of standing guard in the little foxhole. I worked myself to the fireplace as closely as I could. But everybody was standing there, holding his mess kit close to or even over the fire. Food had been sent, and as usual it was cold. I found a few pieces of bread and dumped them in the soup. Ice crystals - as usual - had been all through the bread.

The bunker was now crammed with soldiers, their faces being eerily illuminated by the flickering flames.

Somehow the talk had gotten to the subject of officer candidates and how they had done through the years. The discussion was subdued. I had the feeling that the guys were holding back something.

Finally Corporal Konjetzny started to talk. All the other men now became quiet.

"Heller, what you should know...we might as well tell you now. We have had quite a few officers' candidates through the years. Some of them were okay, but others...were too ambitious. They wanted to attack without artillery preparation, without " Ivan" having been softened up. They wanted to be heroes, wanted their Iron Cross immediately."

He paused. It was now very quiet, except for the slurping sound the guys made when they tried to down their soup. And you could hear the crackling and popping of the logs in the fireplace.

Everybody was staring at me. Some had gotten up and grouped themselves around Corporal Konjetzmny and me, as if they expected something important to be said. And it was:

Joseph Konjetzny resumed speaking:

"One year we had two candidates from your town, I remember them well. One of them was very decent, I must say. The other one - Paul, what was his name?" He turned to a soldier standing next to him.

"I think it was...he had a nickname, 'Beanpole'."

I had to bite my lips. That must have been the guy I met when I visited the Pathfinder group of my brother Pat!

"Yes, that was it, Beanpole. Thanks. He was very aggressive and ambitious. At one time he wanted us to attack a Russian position. He did not even have an order to do so. We warned him that the Russians had a lot of grenade throwers there.

But he did not listen. There was a big argument. Finally he jumped up and started to run towards the Russian trenches, screaming 'You better follow me, right now!'

There was a lot of confusion, but nobody went. Then we heard a shot, and that was it. Nobody knows who shot him in his back...you know what I mean.

"Heller, we are good soldiers and have courage. If we had followed him the vicious barrage of their grenade throwers, which followed immediately, would have killed us all. Nobody would have survived. Killed for what? To satisfy his ambition? No, we are just plain soldiers and have the right to live like anybody else. We have jobs, and girlfriends - some of us have a farm to go back to."

Konjetzny had run out of words. There was absolute silence now.

I had to answer him. I took a deep breath. Then I was able to say calmly and without haste; "Guys, you don't have to worry with me. You will be safe with me. I am not that type."

Konjetzny nodded, and some of the other soldiers seemed to murmur approval, and went back to their benches.

Konjetzny reached into his pocket and pulled a cigarette pack out and took two of them out. He offered me one; he even lit it.

There was no way that I would have refused this token of confidence ,even if I did not smoke much at that time I smoked it slowly, looking at the cigarette as a much-appreciated gift. It was.

The tension was gone. Everybody seemed to relax now. I had the feeling that I had "made it" with them,that now I was one of them..

· · ·

But now a thought struck me: Dietz, remember that strange letter my grandmother had shown you, about the death of her oldest son in France during the World War I? Where his friend wrote that they had been made to attack, threatened with court-martial by a furious colonel if they refused. Her son had told his superior that it was not a good time to attack now, before the artillery had a chance to "soften" the enemy. The officer insisted on an immediate attack, though. Some of the soldiers refused to do that, and in the confusion her son was shot in the back, by one of his own men. Even as he showed signs of wanting to resist too?

Soldiers had to defend themselves in World War I just as much as they had to do that now. I understood now my grandmother, who still after many years was heartbroken about this incident, started to cry or went into another room when somebody talked about it

I had found the secret! This was "it"!

I was sure: it was the common soldiers way to defend himself in situations like this, when it had become a matter of life or death, when an overzealous order to attack the enemy was given by officers or maybe some ambitious sergeant.

The men on their own had found a little sense of security, protection against fatal mistakes made by certain overambitious superiors. Maybe that was all they needed. I felt relief knowing that they were not helpless sheep, being led to an unpreventable slaughter, that they had found a way of selfdefense!

Then, why did my grandmother not go back to America,in protest to what happened? No, her two daughters had married in Hamburg. However, she made many trips to New York to stay in touch with her family there.

Oh, Dietz, you never will have the mind of a kill

soldier. You want to find out what the reality, what the truth is. You know some of it now. It is enough,isn't it?

You don't want to kill Russians, or anybody else.

Get out of this mess, if you can do it in an honorable way,Dietz. Get out,if you can!

. . .

Apparently Schwarzenberg did have other things in his mind with which he was going to evaluate me. A Sergeant Herring came over and stated that he and I would go out on a patrol tonight. We were to approach the

Russian lines and find out what was going on, possibly to get a few Russian soldiers.

We went on our way at ten P.M. and carefully crawled under the barbed wire. It was completely quiet. There was not even sporadic rifle fire anywhere.

We crawled in an eastern direction towards where we suspected the Russian bunkers would be. Herring did not seem to be in any hurry. I stayed right behind him. Then he motioned to me to come closer.

"Heller," he whispered, "stay down, keep your head down. Man, there is no need to get killed for nothing. We will just stay here for ten minutes or so and then go back. We will tell them that everything was quiet, that we could not find anything suspicious. I don't know where the mines are, nobody knows."

That was all right with me.

As we were lying there, perfectly still, I could see a large yellowish object behind a group of trees ahead of me. This object was moving, but its shape was unrecognizable because of distortion by the trees. What was that? Some kind of a rocket? No, it did not move that fast. Then I realized it was a gigantic yellow moon, rising fast, much faster here than in Middle Europe. I looked to Sergeant Herring. He had been watching this too. Both of us smiled.

I was impressed with Herring. He had seen the uselessness of this mission too and had acted just as defiantly as I had felt.

We took our time on the way back, but assumed a labored and strained expression when we told the others that it had been a difficult trip through all that snow, but that we had not found anything suspicious, and had not seen any Russian soldiers.

Despite all the hardship I somehow felt cocky. I did not know why. Was this a sign that I was going to crack up? From exhaustion or some fever?

I still had some dreams of being my own self, trying to be different. So I slung my rifle over my elbow, like a guy hunting birds - it gave me a feeling of being a civilian, even here in the foxhole standing guard.

We had been given walinki, felt boots made by the Russians. They kept your feet warm at any temperature, but they were not watertight at all. The officers had German-made walinki, which protected their feet from water. In January, I was told, there always were a few days when the temperature changed , when it got to be so warm that the snow would melt. This could occur within hours, and everybody had to have their leather boots ready to put on immediately. The warm spell could last only a few hours.

Unfortunately that was just what happened, and I was in the foxhole when melted snow started to run into it. I was able to stand high enough with one walinki, but the other one was soaked in a few minutes, and I knew I was in trouble.

When I was relieved and told the other men what happened, they knew what to do. "Get that Walinki off! Get some snow and rub your toes! It does not make any sense, but it works!"

I did as they said, rubbing the toes with snow . I found some dry socks and put the leather boots on. But I knew that my toes were not all right. The next morning I saw that three of them had turned brownish, and there was no feeling in them.

"Rub them again, every hour or so...."

Was I going to lose the toes? I rubbed them with snow again and again. The color did not change, but I thought I had some feeling coming back.

Everyone now was exhausted from the one-hour-on, two-hours-off routine, from diarrhea and miserable food, and from the constant itching from body lice.

I doubted that I could take it much longer. I started to see lines in front of my mind, the same lines I had seen when I was a little kid and had a very high fever. They looked like an electrocardiogram on a dead patient. I fought these lines as hard as I could, gathering all my willpower...and they gradually disappeared.

. . .

It grew so cold that we could not handle our machine guns without our gloves freezing on to them. We wore two or three underpants, several undershirts and double or triple socks if we had them.

Not one day too early and without announcement, another unit relieved us. They came after it had become completely dark. We grabbed our few things and started to leave. The new soldiers were cheerful, aggressive and a little boisterous.

"Men, be quiet!" Konjetzny hissed at them. "Ivan is just about a thousand feet away. Shut up!"

Konjetzny was the last one out of the bunker. We took off as fast as we could, before somebody up there at headquarters would change their mind.

CHAPTER 26

Our company gathered a half mile behind the front line. The moon did not shine. There were many stars in the icy sky. The snow gave a lot of reflection, and we could see fairly well. There was no wind, but it seemed as if the murderously cold air came pouring from the heavens. We still had to be cautious. Nobody dared to talk loudly.

The Upper Silesian boys had a strange, much subdued reunion. They had not seen each other for weeks. The talk was that we would have about ten days in an R&R area, with better food and plenty of sleep. We still were far too close to the front for any movies or shows or girls. If the others felt like I did nobody was much interested in that sort of thing anyway.

We put our backpacks on some sleds and took off. I still was like any infantry soldier and had to march with them. Their marching speed was incredibly fast. The officers accepted anything from skipping and sliding on the snow to outright jogging, which I could not maintain for long. I kept up with them, although I did not really know how, with one foot in a walinki and the other one in a regular army boot. I was tempted to cheat a little and put one foot on the horse-drawn sleds skid, but I could not do that. I did not want to have it better than the others, at least not now.

After about three hours we came to a village, and we were allowed to warm up in several houses, maybe for ten minutes. I was not the only one who was near desperation. Corporal Konjetzny came up to me. "Heller, I have been told that it really is not too bad if you lie down in the snow and fall asleep - for good. It does not hurt and you never know what happens. It is all over."

"But Kon, how do you know that? How can anybody say that? By then they are dead. I don't believe this."

"Well, I don't remember who told me, but they say the faces of all guys who died this way looked very, very peaceful. Well, never mind." He wandered off.

No, I said to myself. This is not the time to throw your life away. You have gone through a lot during the last few years, and it just has to get better.

As we were marching I started to notice chills and fever and a pounding headache. Suddenly I saw a "straight-line electrocardiogram" in front of my eyes again. Don't give up. Don't fall behind! Hang on for life!

Finally we came to the village where we were going to have our rest period. We piled into a large blockhouse, plopped down on a wooden cots and fell asleep as we were.

The next morning I was so sick with chills and fever that I had to report my condition. I was told to stay inside until the doctor could see me the next morning. The other men went out for practice shooting and other drills. Where was the promised rest period?

My mind was foggy, and I was very tired. I fell back to sleep. After a while I woke up, still having chills and feeling feverish. My toes now hurt quite a bit, and the heel had started to hurt again, and I could feel some moisture in the sock.

Across the room on the wall was a large poster with Adolf Hitler's picture. He seemed to stare down on me. The poster had Russian words printed on it. "Adolf Hitler, our leader, who has brought us freedom." What a stupid lie.

What a farce. Freedom for whom? Under Hitler the Russians certainly did not have any. They were treated horribly, like animals. Did they know how their prisoners were treated? What about the "Commissar order", to shoot all political officers, regardless? What about the SD and SS shooting Jews?

And what plans did he have for the Germans? Keep them in his army for the rest of their lives?

. . .

The other men came back from their practice shooting. They were happy, singing, rattling their weapons, but also starting to clean them immediately. They were talking about how well the shooting went, and everybody was trying to get the attention of somebody else who would listen to their tale of their excellent marksmanship.

I like these guys in a way, I thought. I have learned to understand them, but this cannot be all! There has to be a future beyond soldiering and shooting and standing guard and eating lousy food!

I could not stand it any longer. I pushed myself up on the cot and screamed into the noisy room; "It is not right that you run around like trained killers...with your machine guns - you are too young to be nothing but killers...it is not right that you are happy with this type of life! This can't be all! We have attacked Russia, and that was wrong! Hitler broke his non-aggression pact, showing that he is a liar, and we have been forced to go along with him. We have broken a pact...we have...."

I fell back on the cot, exhausted.

Probably only a few soldiers heard me, maybe it was too noisy with everybody chatting loudly.

But Lieutenant Schwarzenberg had been standing close by, surrounded by a number of soldiers. I saw him turn white, and he bit his lips. Then he parted the circle of men and came over to me.

"Heller, I heard what you just said." He paused for a moment.

"I will...I will personally make sure that you will never wear the cloth of a Nazi officer ,you can be sure". Then he turned away. But he did not act like somebody who was really sure of his own words. Maybe he wondered what I really wanted to say., maybe he thought I was an anti-Nazi. It was clear that he had something else on his mind, which made him speak haltingly, without much assurance. What was it? Could it be that he somewhat agreed with what I had said? He certainly could not admit that. Had I uncovered a deep split between Nazis sympathisers and the traditionalists, who loved to be army officers, but did not like the Nazis?

I did not care at this point what was going to happen. If they had shot me I would not have minded so much. It had been such an unbelievable relief to speak up...finally.

I felt freer than since a long, long time, and I felt closer to eternity than ever in my life. The picture of Pat, my older brother, who always had been against the Nazis and their war tendencies, had suddenly appeared in my mind for a few seconds. He seemed to nod approval.

Why did Schwarzenberg say, "you will never wear the cloth of a Nazi officer? Instead of German or Prussian officer." It sounded somewhat strange

But hold it! Yes, that was it:

For men like Schwarzenberg there never had existed anything else but the venerable German army, nucleus of military power and ambition since King Frederick the Great. Other officers like Lieutenant Hornberg must have felt the same way. He had refused to wear the new, slick ,black uniform of the tank troops because Nazis had designed it. He had insisted on wearing the field-gray uniform. That was his silent protest against the new Nazi elements that had infiltrated the armed forces and were humiliating the officers of the proud Prussian tradition. They themselves were waiting for the day that one of them, and maybe a great general, would replace Hitler and throw the Nazis out. Then their time would come, and they would fight glorious battles and live in Berlin ever after. No real Prussian officer would let himself be commandeered by a corporal, no, not in the long run.

And my outburst must have brought up his, Schwarzenberg's, own thoughts: he actually was ashamed of the way the Nazis waged war, but he also could not or dared not to do anything against them.

So, I had of all things become his spokesman, accusing Hitler and the Nazis . I had done what he and others, who felt the same way,had wished they had done ,what they had promised themselves to do one of these days; to regain their honor and pride of being a German officer.

I then figured that he would not punish me for my remarks,- - - and he did not.

Nothing happened. I had the feeling that the most severe punishment in his opinion would be that I never would be an officer. I believed Schwarzenberg was thinking along this line: he thought that I was feeling the same way, knowing that he himself would have been destroyed, if he could not be an officer.

The alternative would have been a long prison term. I was lucky that he did not put me in front of an army prosecutor."

I saw the doctor the next day. He shook his head and sent me back to Germany with louse-born typhus, frost damaged toes, chronic infection of my heel, and severe exhaustion.

A medic packed me in an eskimo sled and covered me with blankets. Two men pulled me to the railroad station. I was very weak and felt as if I was in some kind of stupor, maybe from the "typhus".

Konjetzny and a few men from our troop had come over to say good-bye. Kon shook my hand, smiled in a friendly way and said, "Heller, I hope you feel better soon. 'Mach's gut!' And...come back."

"Mach's gut!" (do well)I wished them good luck.I was so weak and so tired and had a splitting headache. Then I heard the locomotive hiss and puff and whistle. The railroad cars jerked into motion.

I was on my way to Germany.

CHAPTER 27

I looked around in the train car, at the same time fighting the fogginess in my head. I estimated that there were about 20 soldiers, most of them half asleep, or staring blankly, some in obvious pain.

As the train went over switches or uneven stretches, their bodies were swaying or their heads were nodding in the rhythm of the train car. Most of the guys had some kind of wound dressing, either on their arms or legs, or on their chests. One elderly soldier was chomping on his cigar, at the same time apparently trying to give encouragement to a very young soldier. The young guy had lost a part of his right arm.

A sergeant talked to me saying that he was so glad to go home and resume his career as an opera singer. He would not be drafted again, he said, because he had lost part of his left foot.

Over the next ten days we traveled as a group. At night we stayed in some barracks, one night even in a hospital near Lodcz in Poland. At some stops nurses changed bandages, but we never saw a doctor.

Finally we stopped at a lonely railroad station south of Breslau. A rickety old bus was waiting for us. It took a long time to get everybody inside. A number of nurses were there to help.

On top of a hill we saw a hospital. We got food there and even a bed. I sank onto it and fell asleep within minutes.

As I found out soon Branitz Hospital was a large mental hospital, run by the Catholic church. It had been converted into an army reserve hospital.

Something, though, was strange. I never saw a physician, I never was examined. Nurses gave me a bowl to soak my feet in, after I had asked for it. They also gave me sulfonamide tablets.

I took my first shower, I guess, since Berlin. When I checked my skin there were many scratch marks from trying to fight the lice, but also many reddish areas, probably from the typhus.

I was happy that the toes had held up, and no amputation was going to be necessary. The heel was doing better too. Still, no physician had examined me. That was strange. The nuns said the doctors were too busy...

I was transferred to another part of the hospital. Now I shared a room with another corporal, Hans Wanger. He was a few years older than I. He told me that he was suffering from a severe depression, that the lost battle of Stalingrad was so much on his mind. He looked perfectly normal, but I noticed that he wiped his forehead every minute, even if it was not warm in the room at all. He walked around at times, saying "Stalingrad, how could he let this happen..." I was not so sure whether he had not had other depressing problems. But I was not going to ask. Maybe he would start talking on his own.

Something unusual, though, must have happened recently. The Red Cross sisters, who helped out on the ward, and the nuns got together every-so-often, looked around to make sure nobody saw them, and then whispered. They looked so serious and even frightened. What was it?

I asked one of the Red Cross girls what had happened. She answered slowly, "Corporal, I can't tell you...maybe later."

In the afternoon the Red Cross sister came back. "Corporal, I can tell you just a very few things. As you know, this was a private ward for civilian mental patients. Two nights ago they suddenly were evacuated, in the middle of the night...we had no idea...all the patients were taken to the railroad station, packed into cars. But nobody knows where they went! They just are gone! We are so afraid they have been sent to one of these places where..." She stopped and reached for her handkerchief, wiped the tears from her eyes.

"I can't tell you anything more. How could those doctors give permission...."

She abruptly turned and walked away with fast, hard steps.

I looked at Hans Wanger. He was very much irritated, actually he seemed to be on the verge of an emotional outburst.

"...I hate to say that, but I think she is saying the truth. I have heard about those places where they...put those patients asleep, where they actually kill them.

You don't believe it? Well, I tell you something I have not told anybody else yet."

Hans Wanger motioned over to me and we went into our room, leaving the door wide open, so we could see whether anybody else was hanging around.

"Dietz, all this is possible, I mean the train going to some camp where...

"Anyway, I could not help overhearing what you and the sister talked about. You have to understand that I can not say too much. They released me from one of the biggest concentration camps under the condition that I never would talk. I was a guard in Auschwitz for a while, you know, the biggest camp of them all."

I had heard of Buchenwald and Dachau. I had seen the outside of Buchenwald, but I never heard about Auschwitz. That was new for me.

"Auschwitz is not too far away from here. At first there were mainly political prisoners from the earlier years of the Nazi regime, having been transferred from the "Reich". Then they sent Jews and gypsies, and many more Jews. They were told something about resettlement, and they had to work in a large factory. But you cannot imagine how things then changed. The treatment of the prisoners became plainly brutal. They let them work themselves to death, not feeding them. But what then happened was even worse and plainly is indescribable."

He swallowed a few times and apparently was under great strain to control himself.

"Dietz, they...built ovens and started to gas the prisonersw then burn them to ashes! I still can smell the horrible stench, which came from time to time and hung over the camp. Oh God, I can't tell you...no!"

He wiped his forehead again and again. I put my hand on his shoulder. Was he imagining things? What if this was really true? Gassing? Burning them? How could I grasp that!

"Dietz, I...somehow believe what the sister told you about what might have happened to the patients. Oh hell, I can't talk. Excuse me."

He turned around, blew his nose, took out another handkerchief and wiped his forehead again. Then he walked away. But he came back within a minute.

"Dietz, I will tell you this. If you ever have a chance to get out of Germany after the war, do it. Don't even hesitate. I can't imagine what will happen if all this comes to the light.

I myself will try to get to Canada."

This was a horrible revelation. It made my problems with typhus, made all my problems look completely insignificant. In a way it was worse than those prisoners who froze to death - no I could not say that. This was plain barbaric. Germany, where are you going?

. . .

Finally one of the nuns did talk. We knew her from her continuous efforts to convince one of the farmer girls, who cleaned our rooms, to become a nun. It was an almost daily friendly battle. The girl wanted to marry, and the nun ultimately was unsuccessful.

One day when she made her afternoon rounds, the nun stopped as usual and talked for a minute to this man who had been sitting there day after day, not saying one word, staring into an empty space. She said a few words. I could now see a thankful look in his eyes. Then she came over to Hans and me.

"We are not going to talk about anything. But I want you to know that even if there is a lot of frustration in taking care of mentally ill patients, we know they have a mind. We feel it working as if it were in a cage, unable to come through. Some of them have a few lucid days on and off, some of them just before they die. I tell you, during these hours the patients are so thankful for having regained their minds, it makes our hard work worthwhile. Every minute of it."

I could see tears in her eyes. She turned around and left the room.

I paced up and down the hall, not knowing what to feel or think. Maybe the other persistent rumor had been true too, that guards had removed gold teeth from concentration camp inmates.

I had to get more proof; I had to be sure. I knew the doctors would not talk. They would say I was crazy. Hans Wanger, I felt, had said all he could say. He had become withdrawn for a few days and would not talk.

And further proof came, piece by piece.

. . .

Spring had arrived. The warm sun made me want to go outside. My toes had stopped hurting and they looked normal. So, I got up immediately when we were allowed to take walks.

I passed the chapel about which there had been so much talk. The issue was that the farmers of the county had donated ten thousand eggs to prepare a special paint that would last for many years. That caused a lot of unfavorable comments since eggs had been strictly rationed for years by now. Why couldn't they wait until everybody had enough to eat? Was this a power play between the Catholic church and the Nazis?

I heard the nuns practicing hymns in the chapel, preparing for next month's celebration of the Holy Virgin, and one of their most beautiful melodies hung in the air.

I went on, looking for a warm place to sit down. I found a bench that was protected from the wind by a high hedge. A soldier was sitting there by himself, the empty sleeve of the trousers neatly folded up on the side where apparently his leg had been amputated. He was leaning forward, resting on his crutches, an unlit cigarette in his mouth. He was a blond fellow, looked really Nordic - a perfect sample of the cherished German look.

"Got a match, corporal?" he said.

"Let me see." I gave him a box of matches that I happened to have in my trousers.

"Thanks." The soldier lit his cigarette.

"Keep them, I don't really smoke."

"Thanks again." The soldier looked at my uniform.

"You look awfully young to have the Frozen Meat Medal. May I ask how old you are?"

"I am twenty now, was born in 1923."

"Let's see now. You were in Russia in the winter of forty-one to forty-two to get this medal. So, how old were you when you got into the army?"

"I was seventeen, December 1940."

"Did you enlist, volunteer? At that age?"

"Yes, I did, but let's leave it with that."

"Sorry, corporal, I will not ask any more questions. I volunteered too, for the Waffen-SS."

Now he turned fully towards me. "You know, after this," and he pointed to the empty sleeve of his trousers, "I don't care anymore what I say. I stepped on a mine at the Eastern Front. It got my leg, a piece of my butt, and my left testicle."

He laughed sardonically. "Oh yes, I know what you think. It still works; you know what I mean. But it all came from volunteering. I volunteered, and it cost me my leg."

Now I felt like talking some more with this man. I was sure he was a corporal or a sergeant. He was wearing an old army uniform that did not fit him at all - no SS uniform, no decorations.

"I have to tell you what really happened. First I was assigned to an SS unit. We went all over Poland, together with a unit of SD guys, you know the 'security troops', like police. Our job was to round up all the Jews we could find, whole families if possible. We took them out of town and made them dig their own graves. Then they had to strip, men, women, children. Some girls looked damned attractive, I tell you. But they looked at us when we shot them."

He paused for a moment. "They were looking, just questioning, some of them were crying."

I knew this was another step down into the world of horrible excesses committed by the Nazis. But I had to hear the end of it.

"I could not take it, and a few others felt the same way. It is true that they had told us in the beginning that we were not being forced to do the shooting. But it is not easy to say 'No'. We finally did, though. We chose the alternative; to be sent to the front ,to a fighting unit.

You can figure it out, I am sure; that's where I stepped on a land mine.

What do I have now? I have the Iron Cross first class, the Infantry Combat Badge and the Silver Medal for having been wounded twice.

I do not regret having gone away from the killing, no. Why don't they ship the Jews to Madagascar, as they said they might want to do? Killing like this? No!"

He gathered his crutches and got up, surprisingly easily.

"Good talking to you, corporal, and good luck to you!"

"Good-bye, man, and good luck to you too," I replied.

· · ·

I had to find something I could concentrate on, to forget about these problems. They really were going to overwhelm me. Where was some kind of relief from all these reports of cruelties? Where was peace, or success, where was anything positive?

I had been interested in drawing for a number of years. So what, I thought, let's do it again. I got some paper and found a few pencils and started copying pictures of buildings or other objects, whatever I could find in newspapers or magazines.

Hans Wanger's wife and daughter came to visit for a few days. Hans got leave for one evening so he could have dinner with them.

I was already in bed when he returned. He was happy, relaxed, and said that he had a great time.

In the middle of the night, though, I woke up. Hans was groaning and moaning in his sleep, and restlessly tossing around. I watched him by the little nightlight. Hans had told me some time ago that he had stomach problems.

Suddenly he sat straight up in bed. He started to talk in spurts, his voice getting a little louder. "No, no! They can't do that! Jesus, Maria! Have mercy! They are going to be gassed! There, in that building! Don't go! Don't go in there! Oh Jesus! I can't take it any more."

He fell back, still moaning and shaking his head as if he wanted to throw off a bad memory.

I could not understand anything else. He now was whispering. Then he gradually fell asleep, still breathing heavily.

The night nurse came, holding a syringe in her hand. "What is going on, corporal? He did not have an attack of some sort?"

"No, Sister." I did not want Hans to have been interrogated at this time. I knew how sensitive he was about everything concerning his time as a guard.

"I believe he just had a nightmare. He seems to be all right now."

The nurse checked his blood pressure, pulse and respiration and listened to his heart.

"He seems to be okay. Let me know if he gets restless again. I will leave this bell with you. I will come back in a short while anyway. Good night!"

"Good night, Sister."

So, that's what had been going on in Auschwitz. No wonder that Hans had suffered a nervous breakdown. No wonder he had been sworn to secrecy about Auschwitz. Killing with gas; men, women and children? Children too? Is this the place where the train with the Branitz patients had gone? Or to some similar place?

Maybe I should deny all this knowledge and just go along with everybody's thinking, pretending I did not know?

But I did know, and it was now deeply engraved in my soul.

And Dietz, do not blame yourself for wanting to find out. It just is your nature, you felt responsible for your life, and part of that was having to find out what was going on.

. . .

Auschwitz, and then euthanasia of mental patients - I had to get out of here, I said to myself.

I can't stay here any longer. Maybe the next step would be that they would eliminate badly wounded or seriously ill or mentally ill soldiers. I knew I was not mentally ill, Who would make sure that not the wrong guys were sent away? Even if it meant infantry: get out of this hospital!

I had been feeling better and asked to see a doctor to get a release from the hospital.

Finally I was given an appointment with one of the physicians. He looked at my record and checked my toes and the heel, checked my whole body. He asked me whether I felt strong enough, and I said I did.

"Okay, we will get your papers ready in a few days."

I don't know what gave me the courage, but I asked him, "Doctor, what happened on ward 'D', what happened to those mental patients?"

His head jerked up and he stared at me. He did not say anything for almost a minute. Then he answered, his voice being surprisingly husky; "Corporal, you better get out of here - the sooner the better." He slammed his ledger shut, got up and left the room.

I was back to my old philosophy; don't wait for something to happen, stay ahead, keep on going. There sometimes is more safety in taking a risk than in believing that you were safe as things were.

On the way back to my room I saw this man again, who was sitting there day after day, not saying one word. His wife was sitting as his side. I wondered now what this man had gone through, or what they might have made him do.

. . .

Click-click-clack....

I was standing in the gangway of the express train going back to Weimar. The rhythmical clattering of the wheels almost put me to sleep.

The click-click-clack sounded like "deja-vu, deja-vu, deja-vu." Mr. Eppler, he had been so right. Now it had become not only the biggest war ever; it also was stigmatized by horrific crimes against humanity.

I knew I was not the same man any more. I was helpless, unable to find a way to control all these cruelties.

But I had hope left; those Russian prisoners and the concentration camp victims did not. They were gone.

I had been lucky. My soldier's passbook had not been stamped by the infantry at that time. I could --no, I had to go back to the communication troops! Man, was I glad. If Schwarzenberg's message had come to Waldenburg, the infantry base town, it would have meant the end of me one way or the other.

We arrived in Weimar. The railroad station had been bombed the previous night. Some wooden structures still were smoldering. Twisted steel girders and heaps of rubble were all over the station building area, and some debris covered several tracks. I saw a group of about fifteen men in striped garbs cleaning up, removing bricks or pulling away sheets of metal roofing.

These men obviously were inmates from the concentration camp Buchenwald, which was so close. Armed guards with rifles kept them covered. Welcome home to Weimar, Dietz. Weimar - once the capital of a democratic Germany.

I was assigned to the fixed radio station, a part of an emergency network. We were housed in the new barracks on a hill just outside of town. Some grubby, old sergeant was our boss. He was not interested in anything and left us pretty much alone. Most of the time he was in his quarters and drank beer.

Somehow the radio station had developed into a meeting place. Soldiers, even officers, coming from the front or on their way back to Russia, stopped in and chatted, looking for comrades or news from other guys.

Captain Schultz from my old unit stopped in and said hello. He was friendly and promised he would try to get me back to my old outfit.

I could not believe my eyes when I saw Roland Horn. He was returning from his leave and had been asked to take information concerning a new four-roller enigma machine back to the unit. He was very bitter and downhearted, and I knew enough to understand why.

We got together on the lawn behind the station. "What in the hell did you do, Dietz? You were crazy to volunteer for the infantry!"

I had started to think that Roland was some kind of a genius. He had insights that had surprised me at that time, and I certainly took him seriously.

"Roland, how many young guys were sent to the infantry that winter?"

"I don't know exactly. About nine or ten. Two guys from our troup. They were very young and had just recently arrived. There was one from Bass's troup, which is yours. He was very young too, had come shortly after you left. Three from troup six, including Rudolf Steng, who had been there for quite a while - yes, maybe you were not so dumb after all."

"Roland, do you really think that even one of them survived? I don't believe it. I know now how life is with the infantry.

And Roland, what about the war now? What do you know about concentration camps and all these horrible things that are going on?"

Roland looked at me with a whimsical expression.

"Dietz, I know a little bit. I don't want to talk about it. If all this is true...."

"It is, and more than you think."

"Dietz, we cannot talk about it! It will destroy us if we do, because there is not a damned thing we can do about it!" He sure was upset now.

"You mean; just forget it?"

"No, just don't talk about it. They will get you the moment you open your mouth! Dietz, you have the damned obligation to make the best out of your life, not let them take it. You do not want to die for them!"

He was so right.

We had been sitting on a ledge. The only friendly factor in this world seemed to be the warm sunshine, a blue sky and white big clouds.

I knew that I had risked my life once, when I spoke up. Do it again? How? Where?

The rest of our conversation was anticlimactic. Roland told me that a strafing plane had wounded Karl Weber and that he had not returned to the unit yet.

"By the way, Bass is now Master Sergeant, Osten and Smitty are still there, and about everybody is very discouraged...."

Your 'friend' Heinrich von Ellsleben went to the tank troops and is doing very well. Richie Gattorna transferred to the pioneers and now is in Hamburg as a member of a bombsquad, defusing the non-exploded heavy bombs. This way he could stay close to his mother, who was so badly injured. Well, I myself would not have the guts to do that."

"Neither would I, Roland. Please say hello to the guys, I miss them."
I hated to see Roland go.

CHAPTER 28

Despite everything I was now in "civilized" country. I appreciated again simple things like running water, electricity and...telephone. I made a few calls to Hamburg, surprising my mother. She had not heard from me since Branitz. She told me that Signe had left with her family to go back to Sweden.

My mother had seen Wolf Rohrbach's parents, and they had a really hard time adjusting to the fact that he would not come back. My grandmother and she, my mother herself, were doing all right, but were very tired and exhausted.

I looked through my few belongings to find Ulla's address. I found it on a crumbled piece of paper in my billfold. I immediately wrote to her. I wondered whether she was now in Hamburg.

About two weeks later newspapers and radio were filled with horrible reports about extensive air raids on Hamburg. A very dry July had made the city a perfect target for British incendiary bombs, and the eastern section of town had suffered tremendously. The attacks were repeated for a few days. Stories went around that over fifty thousand people were killed or severely burned. The figures went higher and higher. We lived on the west side of town, but even there destruction was unbelievable. And, only very few enemy planes were shot down, an unusually low figure. What was going on?

Now hundreds of thousands of people were homeless, fleeing the city, not knowing where to go. The hospitals were powerless, unable to even take care of a fraction of the casualties.

Hamburg was an inferno.

Somehow I got through on the phone and talked with my mother. She said they were all right, that the worst damage was on the other side of the town. But then her voice grew unsteady. Mr. and Mrs. Rohrbach had been killed in an air raid just a few days before, she said. She began to cry. "It is too much. We can't take it anymore!"

I felt sorry for her. She did not deserve a life like that at all. I wished I could help her somehow.

During the next few days, more and more information came through. The raids on Hamburg had been the worst air raids of the whole war. But something must have made her more vulnerable than usual. What was it?

The city supposedly was hysterical. The district party "chief" and the Mayor tried to call Hitler and have him come and see the damage and talk to the people. The report came through that these officials actually asked Hitler to sue for peace and end this slaughter.

Hitler did not come. He sent somebody else who tried to soothe the population. But the people remained furious.

The Nazi propaganda called these raids inhumane. Well, had they forgotten what the Germans had done to Warsaw, or Belgrade, or London, with daily or nightly raids for over sixty days?

Or Coventry? Liverpool? Rotterdam - while the Dutch were negotiating a surrender, the German planes nevertheless bombed the city into further submission. No, sir - what else do you expect?

Where was Ulla? She probably was in Hamburg. But how could I contact her? I immediately wrote another note to her.

In all this confusion I was ordered to transfer to a place in Hessia to build emergency housing. What nonsense. After that I would be sent to Frankfurt to train as a radio monitor. That was an honor, because only very speedy and efficient men were chosen for this job. It required you to intercept enemy radio traffic, which at times was awfully fast. These messages then were deciphered by other men.

We arrived at the base. It was very peaceful there, and very boring. The sky was filled with contrails of allied planes and German fighter planes. Fleets of bombers were crossing over us on the way to Berlin or Kassel and other places. The Allies had full control of the skies at this time.

Schmerzenborn, the army base in the Hessian mountains also harbored units of a punishment battalion. We soldiers were not allowed to mingle with them. Every morning they marched out into the forest or the fields for exercises and drills, mainly combat drills. They came back in the late afternoon, bellowing Nazi songs with their last breathes. They were being prepared for suicidal counterattacks wherever there was a need. That was their chance to atone for whatever crimes they had committed. At night occasionally we heard the cries of somebody who received "special treatment". We all felt sorry for those men, who were condemned to die one way or the other.

Our job was to put prefabricated barracks together. Digging the basements was the toughest job. We had only shovels and spades to do the job.

Finally I got a note from Ulla, thank God. She said she was okay, that she had been in "my town" during the raids. They all had been given leave, and she wondered whether I could see her in Kassel, where her train was going to stop on the way to her home in the Black Forest.

Great. I could get some time off, if I promised to work overtime after my return.

We met at the smoky railroad station in Kassel. We would have about fifteen minutes while the train added another locomotive for the long climb on the way to Frankfurt.

Ulla looked all right, but she definitely was pale, and she was very nervous. I noted that she smoked one cigarette after another, and that she had some kind of a blank stare every so often.

"Dietz, I am still not over all this, I believe you can understand that. Maybe it helps me if I talk about it.

"The destruction, the firestorm - it was just like they say a hurricane would be, but it was all flames - people were running around, ablaze, human beings burning like torches. They did not know what to do. They jumped into canals or into the Alster River. They would rather drown than burn to death. Dietz, I saw people, charcoaled adults lying on the ground. The firestorm was so powerful that it sucked the people right into it, right into the flames.

"I was on my way to the defense center. Fortunately one of the officers had picked me up. We just made it in time, then nobody was allowed to get outdoors anymore.

"The radar screens, though, were completely blurred, we could not identify any target, any planes. Nobody knew what was going on. We could not give any directions to the night fighter planes or to the anti-aircraft units. We could hear the British planes, though, wave after wave, flying pretty low and dropping incendiary bombs. The commander screamed at the helpless anti-aircraft liaison officers, finally told them to just shoot, shoot blindly and keep on shooting so the population would believe that everything was normal.

"Phone calls came in from all stations, desperate, reporting huge fires, breakdown of water services, electricity...gas lines were on fire. We had our own generator, but all the other people had none.

"The following nights they came again. It was the same all over, fires, fires and fires. The British planes were dropping millions and millions of little aluminum strips matching the wavelength of our radar. It worked for them perfectly well; they blocked the radar completely. Some people nicknamed these strips 'lametta', like Christmas tree tinsel. What a sick sense of humor."

Ulla tried to laugh or maybe smile; it was not convincing. Then she continued to talk, hoping she could get rid of these awful memories that way.

"Some girls in the center had nervous breakdowns, some screamed. some tried to run outside to get it over with, and the officers had to stop them. Most everybody started to smoke, one cigarette after another, not knowing what else to do.

"Dietz, do you know that a few days before this happened several anti-aircraft units had been withdrawn from the Hamburg area and were sent to Italy? Did you know that? That is strange, isn't it? The British must have known about that! What else do the British know?"

"Yes, Ulla, I had heard about it. If that is not damned suspicious, I don't know. The British must have waited for a day like that, and they acted fast, I must say."

Ulla continued.

"We sat there, unable to do our work, unable to leave the center. Where should we go? The whole city was burning. I don't remember when I slept, and what else we did. It was hopeless.

"Afterwards they tried to get Hitler to come and see this inferno. No, he would not want to leave his secure bunker in East Prussia. Why not? What kind of a Fuehrer do we have? Why does he not stop the war?"

She almost screamed. I put my arm around her. She sobbed as she continued.

"Nobody is tough enough to tackle Hitler and his gang. Why don't we women try it? Why don't we women, maybe a hundred thousand of us, march to East Prussia and demand that he stop this killing...now!"

Her eyes were looking right and left, and she was perspiring. All this was too much for her, I could see that.

"I am sorry, Dietz. I don't want to be this way, but I can't help it."

"Yes, I know the German women. They never will go through with this. Once a German woman has sworn loyalty they will never change it, particularly not if a war is going on. They rather will stick it out to the bitter end. They are not revolutionaires."

She is right, I thought. And the SS and Gestapo would be at every railroad station or gathering point, and that would be the end of it.

We were standing close to each other, and maybe a minute or two passed when nobody spoke. Then Ulla had regained her composure and she asked me how I got out of Russia and about my time with the infantry. I told her a few facts, but I kept it to a minimum. I did tell her about Branitz and Hans Wanger, and about the SS soldier. I knew though, that her thoughts were not really with what I said.

Then she talked again.

"Dietz, there is something else that nobody could tell you or write to you; your brother Pat and his wife both are involved with the underground. Lately they have helped some of the officers who escaped from the POW camp in Sagan in Silesia. They have fed them and arranged for them to sleep in a barn in the Black Forest. I can't tell you more. If you have a chance to visit with your brother, ask him cautiously about it. Rudi is involved too. I know you realize that they all could be shot if the word goes out.

"Yes, something bigger than you and me is going on, bigger than our lives. Be careful, though!"

She got a pencil and some paper out and scribbled something.

"Let me give you my address and phone number in Freiburg. Call me if you can, as soon as you can.

"Dietz, they are ready to go now. Good bye! I love you!"

"Good bye Ulla. I love you too. See you...soon, I hope!"

With a tremendous noise the locomotives started up, first spinning their wheels, bathing the whole station with clouds of white steam. Then the train started to roll.

Ulla had jumped on the steps of the last passenger car, waved shortly and disappeared.

So, my brother had worked with the underground. Wow, that was very courageous. I knew that he hated the Nazis, but I did not expect that. I have to find a way to meet him and talk with him.

And Ulla's idea of the hundred thousand women marching on Hitler's headquarters - it was great.

Why was it so difficult to get a ride back to the camp? Were people tired of helping soldiers?

Finally an old truck stopped and picked me up. It ran on methane gas, produced by roasting chips of wood. It was pitifully slow and stank awfully. It took over an hour for it to climb up the road to the base.

I checked in. When I came to my bunk bed, there was a message to call a number in Ziegenhain, a little town a few miles away. In Ziegenhain? Who could be there?

I called. It was Ulla.

"Dietz - I got off the train in Bad Hersfeld and took a bus here. Can you come down? I just want to talk with you. I promise that I will not cry again. You helped me so much by talking to me and listening to me. I have a few questions to ask you. Can you see me here in the 'Golden Goose'? Also - we will have a good time, like in Berlin."

The guard at the gate shook his head when he saw me leaving again ten minutes after I had arrived. But my papers were okay. I had leave until eight a.m.

We made love, maybe a bit more hesitantly than in Berlin. We were so close. But something was different.

Ulla lit a cigarette and we shared it. It got to be dark. We only had a flickering candle that the hotel had provided. All light bulbs had been broken. There were no replacements. Everything was to be saved for the war effort.

Ulla broke the silence.

"What do you think, Dietz," she began. Her voice was quivering. "You and I - can we make a go of it? I really trust you, I like you and your careful and tender way of making love. I believe you also can be a very good friend."

It was very quiet. In the distance, though, I could hear the whistle of a train.

I took a long drag on the cigarette. "Ulla, I know, I have been thinking of us too. It could work out very well - once I know what I want to do, once I have a good job.

"But I have to be honest. There is something else I have not been able to work out yet. Ever since Branitz I have been trying to decide whether I will stay in Germany after the war or not. Remember, I told you about what they did to the mental patients, and the other actions - these things are so deadly, I mean spiritually. The worst thing was that neither I nor anybody else had any control over it except the Nazis. What kind of thinking was that? Plain cruelty! That is not what I believed Germany stood for."

Ulla was silent for a while. Then she said, "Dietz, don't you think that cruelty is part of any war, and of today's life? Think of how Stalin had treated his Kulaks, and how he punished all his officers, even before the war, how he had the Polish officers killed at Katyn. We have to forget about it one of these days, get over it.

"What do you want to do? Get out of Germany? To America? Canada? Australia?"

"Yes, I might do that. And it is not cowardice. The Nazis do not want to listen to any argument; they have only a few answers like concentration camps - for how long? Or if somebody really is defiant they will shoot him. You don't help yourself or your cause by opposing them directly. My dream of having some input - you know, after the war - to try to modify their policies, eliminate excesses and aberrations - that dream has been shattered for good. Things have happened, and I have seen some of it, that just should not happen in any civilized country."

"But they have the third degree in America. They certainly do not touch serious criminals with gloves on. Also, think of the Negro problem in the States, think of the Ku-Klux-Klan."

"You know, all that is not government subsidized lawlessness. Somewhere a man can find a line of defense. In America you are not guilty until proven so.

"Ulla, it would not be fair if I did not tell you about all these doubts. I have not found the answer yet."

Ulla did not say anything for a while. Loud voices floated up from the tavern downstairs though, interrupting the quietness in our room.

Finally she started to speak again. "Dietz, I am trying to understand you. You outlined a pretty tough and lonely road for yourself, I am afraid. I don't know whether I could follow you, as much as I hate the Nazis. Maybe I still believe too much in the good of Germany, all her cultural accomplishments. And I love Freiburg and the Black Forest and my parents and my family.

"Aren't you making it too hard on yourself, dear? Isn't there another solution, maybe a compromise?

"You have changed so much since Berlin. You are different, Dietz. I think your experiences have been too much for you. And I probably can not imagine how I would feel being confronted with problems like that."

I had to think again. It took me a while to answer.

"I wish it would be different. I guess all this has had an effect on me. I...don't believe in Germany anymore."

The last words had come out like a confession. And I knew it was true. I continued.

"Maybe I would have the guts to fight and die for a cause. But I don't want to throw my life away without having some kind of faith or assurance of a life afterwards. Something more than nothingness."

Ulla looked at me in a perplexed way.

"Then you don't believe in an afterlife, I mean of the Christian manner or description?"

"No. As many times as I have tried to be happy and satisfied with their ideas, I never have been given positive faith in them. I never could call myself a convinced Christian."

Again Ulla was silent for a while. Then she crushed the rest of the cigarette in the ashtray.

"Dietz, I did not know we were that far apart. I am sorry. But I love you for what you said and how you said it. Anyway, let's be friends, good friends, okay? Let's stay in touch with each other.

"I feel better now, despite everything. And...if you should change your mind, if you should see a future for both of us, please call me. Let's give it plenty of time."

She found her robe, threw it over her shoulders and got up.

"I think there is a little wine left, Dietz. Let's share it."

There was about half a glass for each of us. We drank it silently. I picked up my few things and slowly stood up.

"Good-bye, Ulla, and I wish you all the luck."

"Good-bye, Dietz, and you know what they say in Hamburg; Tschuess! Adieu, as the French would say."

CHAPTER 29

Finally I was sitting in the train to Frankfurt/Main. There had been one delay after another due to damage to the tracks from air raids. I got my sketchpad out and drew a picture of the man sitting across from me. He was the perfect model, as he was asleep. It turned out to be a good sketch. I liked it. There was no beauty in it, but a pretty strong expression of endless stress and exhaustion.

I wrapped the drawing up and put it away. We were approaching Frankfurt/Main.

A gigantic dark-gray cloud was hanging over the city. For two weeks the city had been bombed every day and every night. The Americans came in daytime, the British at night. At times the population was warned ahead of time where the bombing would take place. The Allies dropped leaflets announcing for instance that tonight the area from the 50th to the 75th street would be bombed, advising the population to get out.

The new training consisted of endless hours of listening to taped allied radio traffic, all in Morse code, to get used to their particularities and their routines. You had to learn to kick in immediately when you felt that a real message would come, write it and forget about the unimportant details. Their transmissions were very fast. We had to learn a new way of speed writing in order to keep up with them.

It had been so good to talk with Ulla a week or so ago. I needed someone here to talk to also. I noticed two men who looked intelligent, apparently were good friends and talked a lot together. Sometimes they talked in a very low voice, as if nobody else should know what they were talking about. I found out that one of them was a lawyer in Munich, and the other one was a young musician in the same town. I picked up a few remarks from the older one, indicating that he was rather critical of the war, stopping short of saying that this war was lost.

On quiet, non-air-raid evenings we went out together, combing the town for some restaurant that offered soup or something else without the need for ration cards.

But nobody dropped his mask and talked freely. How could you?

As the time for our new assignments to active units approached, we were talking more and more about where we would be sent. The greatest probability naturally would be the eastern front. The losses there were much greater than anywhere else.

"I don't know what I am going to do," I told Walter and Heinz. "If they send me there, I don't believe I will make it back. I know too much about what's going on there."

"What can you do?" Heinz said dejectedly." You have to go wherever they will send you. If you make a stink they really will send you to a bad place."

Walter Mueller, the lawyer, was in the same mood. "Yes, Dietz, the less you antagonize these guys the better your chances are. There is nothing else you can do."

I was not happy with their philosophy. Why did they not even try? They were like sheep going to their slaughter.

On the same day I received orders to report to a unit in northern Russia.

I had to do something, now, fast. Before they would put me on a train to Russia! Maybe there were some other assignments available. I have to talk with the Master Sergeant.

I got an appointment to see him the next day.

"With all due respect, Sir,I would like to ask for another assignment. I have been at the eastern front for two years. I request assignment to another front."

Master Sergeant Friedman's jaw dropped. Then he recovered enough to take a long look at me. I knew he himself had been excluded from being sent to Russia because of a heart condition.

At least he did not burst out accusing me of being a coward.

No, his voice was rather mellow. "Let me look at your record," he said. "I will see what I can do for you. That is all. Dismissed."

I returned to the company. They were singing some new songs like "Tampico! At the Gulf of Mexico" and "Inge, Du alleine sollst in meinem Herzen sein."

A few hours later a messenger came from the Master Sergeant's office. My assignment had been changed. I would be sent to Athens, Greece, instead.

Hallelujah! Man, I had not even used graft or connections. At least there was no fighting in Greece right now, and the Allies were not far away.

A day before I left for Greece a letter from Ulla arrived. She still wrote about Hamburg and the air raids, but then particularly about Rudi, whom she had seen quite a few times when she was in Freiburg. He had lost several toes in the winter in Russia, and after a long time had regained his ability to stand and walk. He had been discharged from the army and was looking forward to a teaching assignment at the University of Freiburg.

It was obvious that both of them would make a good team, I thought. I predicted that they would get married. Ulla certainly had marriage on her mind.

Why not? His affairs soon would be settled, and mine? I felt like a vagabond. I had accomplished nothing as far as my own future was concerned.

It was good to be back in a subtropical climate. The sun shone all the time, and white, fluffy clouds were in the sky. And - we were far away from Russia.

But that was only one point. I could feel the restlessness here. German soldiers had been shot on the bus to Athens. Partisans were all over. They even used wire fences to transmit their telephone messages. How we found out about it officially was a well-kept secret; but we knew that some guy had hooked up his receiving equipment to one of the wire fences, just for fun, just playing around.

We were about twenty miles away from Athens. We rarely had a chance to go there. On those days when I did I noticed that the population was very unfriendly. Why shouldn't they be? But I managed to see the Akropolis, even attended a concert in the open theater next to it. While we were listening heavy planes flew over this area and destroyed any attempts to appreciate the music.

We had almost no contact with the Greek people. The bilingual station Radio Athens claimed that the Greek people actually had been freed by the German troops. Freed from what? The German propaganda had tried to tell the same story to the Russians.

We lived and worked in a very large sanatorium, that originally had been built for tuberculous children. Nobody knew what happened to them. The saying was that they were just sent home. It was built halfway up on a mountain, the Pentelikon. We had an unbelievable view over to the Aegean Sea and the surrounding mountains. The highly elevated position allowed us to receive radio messages from far away like from Africa, Italy and even Southern France.

At night we listened frequently to Radio Belgrade. Most of the guys could not get enough of the "Lilly Marlen" song. The station played it every night. To me this song sounded so creepy, so over-glamorizing a soldier's life that I could not help asking, "Do you guys really like this song? It makes a soldier's life sound so romantic. I mean, by now we all know that it is not this way. Think of all the losses, of all the guys who got killed."

"You are too critical, Dietz," Fritz Engelheim said. "Why don't you just enjoy it. One of these days you will understand that a lot of guys like it and get something out of it, even if you don't."

I did not want to argue with him. I could have said: You guys like it and fall for all that soldier's stuff, and that's why you are here or in Russia, doing and accomplishing what?

The word was out that volunteers were needed to man a listening post on a small island near the Turkish mainland. Allied troops were known to be in Turkey, and we had to find out what was going on. The volunteers were to be flown by glider to the little island.

I volunteered and had to participate in a special course where we were trained in even more specialized items of the British radio traffic. Maybe there was a way to get myself captured by the British.

Suddenly this plan was canceled, and now for the first time we heard talk that we would evacuate Greece. The eastern front had started to crumble, and the German troops were too widely dispersed.

We left Greece. Our unit was badly decimated in an air raid and subsequently dissolved. I was assigned to another company in Austria. That's where I met Karl Weber. He had suffered severe wounds in an air attack and had been re-trained to be a radio monitor.

I was so glad to see him and we talked for hours. He had bad news from my old unit: Roland had been taken away by the Gestapo, apparently he had some connections to the underground. They even knew that he had seen me a few times. When they heard that I had volunteered for the infantry, they abandoned the search for me. No anti-Nazi would ever volunteer for the infantry. Karl said that they never heard from Roland again. He also told me that he still had some problems with his right leg, it really had not healed fully yet. But he was as friendly and as cheerful as he could be.

"By the way, you missed out on the great heroic deed performed by Sergeant Roemer. You would not believe it: Captain Schultz and Lieutenant Hornberg had tried to make an officer out of him and they were going to send him to officer's school. But somehow they thought he would be better off with a decoration, like the Iron Cross. Well, they arranged for a trip in the MTW, the troop carrier vehicle, to the front - no, to a point five miles away from the frontline. Roemer then operated the cannon and shot a magazine or two into the empty forest - no Russian within five miles; turned around and drove back to our village. Yes, he had proved himself under "dire circumstances and shown exceptional courage"...ha ha ha. The soldiers laughed or got really mad, and he was told never to come back to our unit. He went, and I don't think anybody heard from him, maybe his friends Schultz and Hornberg. They were all the same: they were not Nazis, but fanatic Prussian-army purists. The sad thing was that there was no Prussian army any more.

Spiritually it had died on the day we entered Russia.

Hitler then killed himself. But what did he do before that? He appointed Admiral Doenitz as his successor. I could not believe that. Just nine months previously the officer's corps had tried to kill Hitler. Now he chose an officer as his successor? Not one of the party members like Himmler or Goering or Borman!

Hitler, you again completely denied your Party! You completely denied your own "revolution"! You showed that your Party only had been your tool: Your tool to grab the power for the militarists.

It was sickening.

Then really bad personal news came through. My brother Pat was very sick with a heart infection. He was in a hospital near Hamburg and was not expected to live. They had no medicine for this disease. His former teacher, Professor Bartel, tried to get some of the new wonder drug penicillin from Switzerland. It was going to be very difficult, they said.

Rudi and Ulla had married. I was not that upset, I had seen it coming. On one occasion, though, I became a little sentimental. That was when one of the soldier's wives wore the same perfume like Ulla had used.

Well, it had been a great time in Berlin. I imagined that I could hear the song of those days, which I still liked very much: "Bei Dir war es immer so schoen."

Then I received a telegram that my brother had died.

A few friends and I later on, after the armistice had been declared, walked from Klagenfurt north across the Alps and were held by the Americans as prisoners-of-war for two weeks. Finally I found a train and went back to Hamburg.

BOOK THREE

California Crossroads

CHAPTER 30

The city of Hamburg was horribly destroyed. When we arrived at the main railroad station, I started to realize how bad it was. The roof was gone. The remaining steel frame was twisted badly and reached into the sky like a surrealistic sculpture. The area around the station was in ruins, with crumbled half-walls and chimneys jutting from mounds of rubble. Everywhere it was the same.

As the train rolled slowly towards Altona I could see again nothing but ruins and rubble, burnt out houses and leveled warehouses and factories.

Finally I was in the tramway riding towards our suburb. I looked up and down in the tramway car. All passengers looked haggard, badly nourished and badly dressed - and stoical. I did not recognize anybody. Most of them carried some packages or knapsacks. They probably had been in the countryside trying to buy food.

The old tramway lumbered around a corner and climbed slowly up a hill on top of which a very large windmill had stood for many years. It was gone. Some charcoaled ruins told the story.

We passed a park on the right side. For many years it had been called the "Rathenau Park," named after a courageous politician, who had tried to pull Germany together after World War I. He was assassinated by fanatic nationalists who did not like the fact that he was a Jew. The Nazis did not like him either and renamed the park after two of their fallen street fighters.

The tramway now gathered speed down the Luetzowstrasse. Suddenly it came to me: Luetzowstrasse, Moltkestrasse, Wrangelstrasse, von Rhone Allee, Walderseestrasse - all were named after former generals, war heroes of 1870 or before or after. These were the men we had been raised to admire and emulate.

Then I got out of the tramway. But what was that? Every tree near the tramway stop was plastered with notes: "Erna Klein, we are now in Barmbeck, Bluecherstrasse #9. Please see us!" or "Heinz Bauman, age 18, last in Stettin. Has anybody seen him? Please contact Olga Bauman...."

And so on. No, there was no mail service yet: hundreds of thousands of homes had been obliterated, and only a few telephones had been restored.

Since I was here last, many more houses had been destroyed. I was now very apprehensive,and I could feel my heart beating very fast But then I could see our house. It was intact, thank God, except for the long crack from the basement to the roof. What a relief.

I walked around the house to the back entrance, which we always used. I passed the garage, where I could see my grandmother's Opel car, almost completely hidden under broken sheets of drywall.

I rang the doorbell, but the door was open and I walked in. My mother came rushing down the steps. "Hi, how are you? I have to see Mr. Punsch right now. See you in a short while..." Off she went.

Well, I had called her yesterday from Harburg, and she knew I was coming. I am not for great dramatic scenes, but I wished she had stopped a minute or so to make me feel welcome. After all, the last few years really had not been a picnic for me.

What was so important about Mr. Punsch? I knew he was one of the displaced persons who lived in our house now.

I made up my mind in a few seconds. I knew I had to stay here, but I was not going to stay here one minute longer than I had to. I had decided not to open old wounds and be cooperative in view of my brother's recent death, and all these terrible circumstances in the city and in all of Germany. But after this reception, I was not so sure anymore.

I threw my backpack down and stomped upstairs to see Inge and the baby.

Inge and the baby were in the big bedroom upstairs. We embraced. I had to look at the beautiful baby girl. She was sleeping. I could see a few strands of her silvery hair.

Later on I talked with Inge.

"I am so sorry, Inge, about Pat." There was not much else I could say. I noticed her bitterness when she started to talk. She courageously overcame all attempts to cry: "Pat - Pat had septic endocarditis, you know, infection of the heart. But he did not have to die. His teacher had succeeded in smuggling the new wonder drug Penicillin from Switzerland, just about enough to cure him. What a blessing, I thought. Pat always had good friends. Then I overheard the nurses say that his doctor was going to use the penicillin for another patient! I ran to him and questioned him. He said that the chief surgeon had ordered this. The other patient was a famous colonel in the air force who had a severe leg infection."

"Inge - that is horrible!"

"Well, the doctor also said that they knew that Pat was connected with the underground, that he had helped British prisoners, who had escaped, helped them to go to Belgium, and that they knew that Pat had some other health problems." She started to cry.

"They said that it was more important to cure a war hero than a man who was not...fighting for the great cause. So, they took his penicillin and gave it to the colonel. They said they were trying to get some more as soon as possible.

I was furious. What had happened to these doctors?

"Inge, I can't believe that. . .but no, I can believe it, because I know of similar actions, when helpless patients were...eliminated." It was like Branitz hospital all over again.

I told her then about Branitz and the mentally ill patients.

It was a horrible homecoming. Inge then said that she had put in a complaint and that the medical society had answered, promising that the surgeon would stand trial.

I knew we all had to stick together to survive the coming months. There would be almost starvation rations, there would be a question whether we could make it financially, and the Russian troops were about forty miles away in the East German zone.

CHAPTER 31

I was very fortunate to be admitted to the Medical School. But the money that I had saved during the war was running out fast. I had to resort to the black market a few times to buy food. It was dangerous since I could be expelled from medical school if I were caught. Hundreds of other men were waiting on the sidelines to get in.

They promised me that once I was a Junior I could apply for a scholarship. I had to stick it out until then.

Gradually everything became a little easier. Mail was being delivered, at first at irregular intervals. My grandmother made contact with her sister and brothers in New York who started to send "Care"(food) packages.

I got a card from Signe. In a way I wished I had not heard from her. To go through all that again? What did she want? Would I have to play the role of the "second choice?" I decided to see her, but to be very careful.

She was coming to Hamburg twice a week as an airline stewardess for the SAS, a Swedish airline. They were preparing regular service to Hamburg and London. She wanted to meet me at her hotel in downtown Hamburg.

The "Four Seasons" Hotel was one of the few hotels that had survived the war fairly well. They had made necessary repairs. When I entered the foyer I was impressed by the beautiful and elegant restoration, which made you forget that there had been so much destruction.

Signe came down after a very short while. Did she ever look radiant - like a goddess, who just had come down from her place in heaven. Her walk was so graceful, so light and springy. Her beautiful hair was almost as long as she had carried it previously, and her smile tore me apart. I forgot all the questions I wanted to ask and all the problems I wanted to discuss.

She simply said "Good to see you, Dietz!" and everything was like on the day we had taken the trip on my motorcycle to the Elbe River.

Later on we talked for a long time. I told her about my experiences in the war, and that I was thinking of emigrating to the USA. I told her about Branitz and other occurrences.

I also thought I would grab the bull by its horns and said that I still admired Wolf but that I did not like what happened later.

Signe told me about Sweden, and said that she understood me, since they had heard about Auschwitz and other cruelties too, and that she did not blame me that I felt that way.

"Signe, presently I have nothing much to offer, but it should be different in a few years. That's just the way it is...."

She did not answer, but got up and kissed me. It was wonderful. Then she said, "Dietz, we are adults now. Why don't you stay with me when I am in town?"

"By the way, do you still have those pictures of me?" I loved the way she could assume her mischievous look so fast. I found some remnants of her nude photo in my billfold. Not much was left, having been exposed to rain, snow, heat and frequent handling. When she saw those fragments she broke out in a delightful, earthy laugh and clapped her hands. I could not keep myself from joining her laugh.

"So, you'll stay, Dietz?" she said. "Say, yes!"

Signe's trips to Hamburg were the biggest bonus I had since a long while. We got along so well, and those times in her hotel were highlights of my life, especially since everywhere else so many problems had to be dealt with.

What really bothered me was that hardly anybody even now talked against the Nazis. It was as if their deeds and thoughts were so much of the history of Germany that nobody really dared to separate himself from it. The other point was that generally times were so harsh that nobody felt like analyzing or dealing seriously with the past.

I met some high school classmates, who still did not want to admit anything but defeat. Everybody commits cruel acts during war, they said. There was nothing wrong with the treatment of the Russians. See what they did to the German women after the world war! Well, I thought, who had started the whole mess? What was done to the Russian civilians? You don't remember?

Concentration camps, slave labor camps - they were necessary evils of war, they said. Cruelties? See what the Turks did to the Armenians after World War I!

Nobody brought up any real hatred, anger or shame for what had happened. Very few people really followed the Nuremberg trials. Many people believed the stories about gassing and killing of Jews and other unwanted "elements" were vastly exaggerated. What? I thought. One of the factories that had produced the deadly Cyclon-B gas was right here, twenty miles or so east of town.

I found out that the idea of "eliminating" mentally ill patients was nothing really new in Europe. Several authors had written about it. But only one group did it: the Nazis. It was run by a number of men living in Berlin, working at the address of Tiergartenstrasse four: that's where the code name T4 came from. Besides temporary protests by some clergymen, this program was followed through after all.

A former good friend came back from a prison camp that contained only former SS officers and soldiers. They had been fed very well: there had been some plans to send these men to fight Russia, together with Patton's troops. He said that they all had become friends, were going to stay in touch with each other together and one day would rebuild something like the Nazi party.

I hoped that these men would change their minds. But their determination worried me.

It became clear to me that I never wanted to have a family in Germany. I had seen too much, and experienced too much,and I was afraid that this whole mess might be created one day again.

I received a short note from my friend Nolle's mother. Her son was going to come home after 4 years as a prisoner in Karaganda in Russia, having worked most of the time in a coal mine.

Was she ever happy. Four years of waiting, not knowing from one day to another whether he still was alive! And she must have heard all the other reports of prisoners having been starved to death, or, as it was a common occurrence, falling down the icy ladders in the mines, where there were only a few elevators.

I had called her from time to time, just to show my interest. She certainly appreciated that.

A few days later I met him. He looked pale and waxen, and his face was swollen. He had used the salt method: you ate a lot of salt, even put it in your rectum. Your body then would swell to resemble hunger edema. You became useless as a miner and were sent back to Germany. But you risked your kidneys in this gamble. A good number of prisoners became deadly sick with kidney disease and did not make it.

What really was upsetting, though, was that he had become a communist. He talked like one, quoting Marx or Lenin and trying to convince me that their aspect of European history was the true one. He now despised European civilization, had lost all faith in it.

Something had to be done. I called a meeting of all remaining classmates at our house to talk with Nolle and straighten him out. I could get seven boys together, including Klaus Rieder who himself had come back from Russia a few weeks earlier. We had to settle for pop and coffee. I did not have enough money to offer beer or wine.

Nolle was very stubborn. All of us tried our best. His mind seemed to be absolutely set. He insisted on his pro-communist views

After an hour or so Kurt Vogel came. He had survived the war safely as a medical officer at the St. Nazaire submarine base. I moved over to him. I had a few questions.

"Kurt, whatever happened to Mr. Zeller, the janitor at our high school? Remember how he predicted at that time already that there would be a World War?"

"Dietz, the news is sad," Kurt replied. "He finally was drafted after all. He went into the "Volkssturm," the last ditch brigade made up from all the very old and the very young soldiers. They were sent to the Rhine River to stop the Americans...what a crime. Zeller then was shot because he had encouraged the young ones to lay down their weapons, that it was useless to fight any longer.

Quite a man, Dietz, don't you think so?"

"That is just horrible, Kurt," I said. I still saw him with his cigar rolling between his lips, giving us young ones information we certainly first did not want to hear, and who gave us all the predictions which we certainly did not want to accept at that time.

"Have you heard anything about Prinzhorn, our German teacher? Somebody said that he was jailed a few times because of anti-Nazi remarks he had made."

"That is true, he was in jail a few times. He was made principal of our school recently -- that is at least some compensation for all his trouble. Do you know that my father was made principal of Altona high school? You remember that he had been fired, then rehired, then fired again because he was a Social-Democrat? He has stuck it out, he won his battle."

"I am glad for him, I admire him. Just like Mr. Schroeder, who suffered quite a bit too.

Tell me, Kurt...have you ever heard any details about Wolf Rohrbach's ship, its loss?"

"Dietz, - one of the officers of Wolf's first command, the "Piranha," told me quite a story. Wolf was transferred for disciplinary reasons because he had refused an order of his commander to shoot at a boat with shipwrecked allied sailors. I do not know the circumstances, but this could have been mutiny. As you might remember, his second ship, Captain Unger's boat, then was lost a few days later on. I wish I would know more about all this, but Wolf is dead, so are all crew members. Nobody has heard from anybody."

I hardly could contain myself. Wolf had refused to kill shipwrecked sailors? That would be great. That would be just like the same Wolf Rohrbach who had stood up and protested against us singing that Nazi song on our boat trip! Our pact! Yes, he had fulfilled it! Never mind what happened with Signe and him.

A few weeks later I did meet Nolle. He told me sheepishly that he had a change of mind and had enrolled in the pharmaceutical college. Actually, he was quite content and thanked me for getting everybody together. He was trying to forget about those horrible years in a Russian prisoner-of-war camp.

I ran into Birgit Hammer, Guenther's sister. She had her little daughter with her.

"Dietz, do you remember Allan, our exchange student from Liverpool?"

"Yes, I sure do. He was such a nice guy. What about him?"

"Allan stopped in a few days ago. He is now a sergeant in the British Occupation force and is stationed just east of town. You know, he still is the same: very careful not to get involved in any argument. But I told him that Germany would bounce back, that we would be on top again in about ten years, and that we would be the winners of this war after all."

Then she added with a determined look, "I also told him that we were not the first ones to have used concentration camps, that the British used them in the Boer Wars. Well, after that I don't think he ever will come back again to see us!"

She said this with a very self-satisfied expression.

"Birgit–"

"Yes, Dietz, that's the way we all feel in our home, and I let him know it."

"You don't think you were a little rough on him? After all, he was nice enough to stop in and see you, and he knew that you were pretty fanatic Nazis!"

"No, I said what I thought. We will make it, we will build up a great Germany again."

Then she added. "By the way, Guenther will have to go back to Harbor Hospital. He is not doing well, and they are afraid that his tumor has spread. I understand you will take an externship at Harbor Hospital for a few months. You will take good care of him, won't you?

I have to go now. Tschuess!"

She picked her daughter's hand up and dragged her along.

One day we were dissecting a corpse in anatomy. All the corpses reportedly were from Russian prisoners, having been stored in the freezers of the department of anatomy for a long time. A good number of them had been decapitated. Students of brain or facial anatomy probably had used the heads.

Our teaching fellow carefully opened the abdomen and proceeded to explore the stomach. He opened it very carefully. Suddenly we saw with horror that the whole stomach was filled with undigested leaves and small branches of bushes. Apparently this man desperately had tried to find food - any food.

It was absolutely quiet at our table. The girl student, who had been working with us, turned around as white as a bed sheet. She brought her hand up to her mouth and started to retch. Then she began to walk out, unsteadily, holding on to tables or chairs. We never saw her again.

This was "it" for me too. It was the day of my final decision to get out of the country, no matter what. I also had learned to understand why so many young men had left Germany , especially in the nineteenth century. If they did not leave they would be drafted and sold to Dukes or Kings like the King of Bavaria. Well, having sold him about ten-thousand men

Napoleon made him a king. Only about fifteen hundred men returned. Dietz - don't you remember the monument in Munich which honored these ten thousand men?

Our phone still had not been reconnected, but the radio had started to go back on the air. We had electricity for a few hours every day. Listening to the local news I was startled when I heard the name Richie Gattorna. He was the leader of a bomb squad. They were named to receive an award from the Mayor for their courageous work defusing bombs. There still were quite a few bombs around, and the builders restoring houses found some here and there. The work of the squad would continue, but their leader Richard Gattorna had retired receiving high honors.

Richie had survived! He must have a phone, and I tried to get his number from the mayor's office. Yes, he was listed and I made a call from the post office. He was so happy to hear from me, said that he was sure that I was lost in Russia.

We got together and talked out heads off for most of the night. He was satisfied with life, said that he had saved some money and was planning to buy a car agency like Mercedes or BMW. I should not worry about him, he had finished his job. He never was going to touch a bomb again. After I told him about my plans he said that I was crazy to immigrate to America.

I didn't want to complain, but studying was rough. We had no books, and you had to copy information every day from the blackboard. Finally some enterprising guys made paperback copies of some of the textbooks. Transportation - no cars, no motorcycles. There was no gasoline. We jumped from busses to elevated trains - and walked a lot. Classrooms were mostly unheated and overcrowded. There was no other philosophy but: stick it out or give up.

Occasionally I heard from former friends or comrades. I also had wondered what every happened to Heinrich von Ellsleben. He had said the last time I saw him that he wanted to go to the tank troops and see some action.

He actually got into the "Panzerlehrbrigade", a unit which trained tank troops. Apparently he did very well later on and earned the Knight's cross by destroying twenty-five Russian tanks. He was very proud and told everybody about his accomplishment.

But something was fishy. There were rumors of an investigation. It was found out that he only had destroyed twenty-one tanks. Some of them were previously destroyed Russian tanks, on which they poured gasoline and then blew them up..

The twenty-fifth tank also had been damaged before. There were two Russian girls and a German sergeant inside, having a good time. They got out, yes, but some of them had severe burns.

The army would not tell, but he never received another promotion.

Heinrich - who had been such a coward in our encounter - what gave him the strength to be such a hero now? Was it the thought of fighting for Germany, for the great Third Reich, for the Fuehrer? Or was it the burning desire to show that he was not a coward after all - I did not know, and I did not really care.

CHAPTER 32

Two weeks after I had met Birgit Hammer, her brother died at Harbor Hospital.

His memorial service was held on the following Tuesday, a chilly and dreary November day. A fine drizzling rain had started and made it even more depressing.

I was late, having been held up at the hospital, and the funeral home was crowded. I had to find a place in the back. Before the war this funeral home had been one of the most beautifully furnished places in the city. I had been here for my aunt's funeral. Now, despite some courageous attempts to deal with bomb and fire damage, it still was obvious that part of the wallpaper was charred. Other areas showed destruction from water having run down the walls. Crude plywood sheets could cover only some of the many holes and gaps. There was a sour smell in the rooms, a smoky smell I knew well from the time in Frankfurt, when we tried to stop fires after air raids.

I did not know that Guenther Hammer had so many friends. The men outnumbered the women by far. Most of them had short haircuts and wore clothing that had been part of some uniform before. I figured that these men must have been his fellow officers. I realized then that these men had come to honor their friend and comrade, but they were also using this occasion just to get together. The British occupation forces had forbidden any assembly of officers or soldiers except for funerals and similar occasions.

I noticed a tall man, obviously a former officer, with rigid facial features - that was Ludwig von Kronebach, Guenther's commander on the Piranha!

I had seen pictures of him during the war years, and who could ever forget the eagle-like expression in his face and especially in his eyes?

I remembered also that there had been talk that he now was a high-ranking officer in the STASI, the East-German security service. Next to him was a man who also very well could have been an officer. He looked around nervously, scanning the assembly over and over.

This would be my chance. I would get to von Kronebach and ask him about Wolf, yes! Calm down, Dietz, and make your move in time, I said to myself.

The service started with a hymn. A few keys of the organ were pitifully out of tune, and some others produced only a scratching sound.

I stole a look at Guenther Hammer's mother. She looked composed and calm, almost smiling. How things had changed in her life. Her husband had been killed at the Yugoslavian front, her oldest son Ossie had died in an infantry skirmish in Russia. Now her second son had died.

The service was very short. I saw von Kronebach approach Mrs. Hammer and start to talk. I began to work my way towards both of them through the crowd. Von Kronebach now shook hands with Mrs. Hammer, bowed his head, and I thought I could hear him clicking his heels. As he was turning away from Mrs. Hammer I intercepted him.

"Excuse me, sir - may I talk with you for a minute?"

"What is this about? I have very little time!"

Von Kronebach eyes me suspiciously. I continued.

"My name is Doctor Heller. I was one of the attending physicians to Captain Hammer. Shortly before he died he spoke of a serious difference of opinion on his boat, between you and a certain Ensign Wolf Rohrbach, who was my best friend. Guenther Hammer said that the incident then..."

Von Kronebach had turned red in his face. He stared at me as I continued. "...necessitated a disciplinary transfer of Ensign Rohrbach to another submarine - which was lost a few days later. Guenther Hammer felt guilty and not guilty for having arranged this transfer."

"Doctor," von Kronebach swallowed a few times, "Doctor, I have nothing to say, nothing whatsoever. All this happened years ago. A war was going on, you might remember!"

His expression changed and showed some haughtiness. Even his voice was different now, and he sounded like an officer giving somebody a reprimand.

"For us, with whom Ensign Rohrbach served, for us this man is dead. The German navy has no room for mutineers and cowards! Good day, Doctor."

He started to turn away from me, but suddenly reversed his direction and added in an even more contemptuous tone, "I hope your intelligence service is as good as ours. We know that he survived when his U-boat was lost, and we know that he was in an American prison camp until he escaped and probably went to Canada. He simply was not worth to be an officer in the German navy."

The man who had been standing next to von Kronebach now spoke up in an urgent voice.

"Herr von Kronebach, please! We have to go right now! The director does not want to wait for us!" He actually tugged on von Kronebach's sleeve, almost getting him off balance.

I understood clearly. The man was a watchdog for von Kronebach. Maybe his superiors in East Berlin were afraid that he would defect to the West.

Von Kronebach shot a hateful look at him, angrily brushing the man's hand from his sleeve.

"I will go when I am ready, Herr Kapinsky."

Then he turned again toward me.

"There is nothing else I can tell you, Doctor. Good day."

He followed Kapinsky. His face was flushed with anger and embarrassment, but he nevertheless followed him. Like a whipped dog will follow his master, even right after a whipping.

Was that the proud Commander Ludwig von Kronebach, once a fearless and brilliant submarine skipper?

Wolf in Canada? Survived the loss of his U-boat? My heart raced. But why did he not write? Maybe he was brain damaged and could not communicate? But he had escaped from a POW camp - all kinds of thoughts tumbled through my mind. Could somebody find out whether he was alive? Who? How?

After a while I relaxed. To me this man von Kronebach must have suffered from a nagging conscience. What else could have forced him to look for information on Wolf? Wolf had nothing to do with East Germany.

Mrs. Hammer had asked me to stop in at a reception at her house following the funeral. I really had not felt like going, but now it was different. Maybe there were some officers who could tell me more about what had happened on the Piranha.

As expected there were quite a few men who undoubtedly had been officers. After having talked to Guenther's family, I worked myself close to a group of men who were talking excitedly. It was all war talk.

"Gentlemen, I wonder whether some of you can help me get some information on a friend of mine, Ensign Wolf Rohrbach, who reportedly perished on Captain Unger's boat - sorry, I don't know it's number. Now I hear that he may have survived."

It was as if somebody had mentioned the name of a deadly enemy of the State. All conversation stopped. Everybody stared at me, and nobody said a word.

Finally one gentleman, who seemed to be older than the others, shooed me away, taking my arm gently.

"You have come upon a very touchy subject, sir. Do you really need to know?" he said with a somewhat worried expression on his face.

"Yes, I want to know. My friend I understand might have survived and possibly was in a POW camp, then escaped." I said.

"Nobody wants to mention this particular ship. A lot of former submariners know that it was captured, not sunk, and that the new coding machine and codes were captured also. It was very suspicious that the Allies now suddenly could read our code again, while they had been unable to do so for a few weeks, ever since we introduced a modification of the Enigma coding machine. I am sorry, but do you know by any chance what I am talking about?"

"I am familiar with the Enigma. I worked with it a lot during the war. I was a radio operator."

"Oh, good. Then you understand. Many former U-boat men feel that this was the end of submarine warfare. Most of them think that Captain Unger or somebody on the boat should have blown up the Enigma machine and the codebook. Now Admiral Doenitz had to call many boats back. The losses had skyrocketed.

I don't want to be intrusive, but I advise you not to mention Captain Unger anymore. I could not have told you this even a year ago.

Good talking to you. See you!"

Now I could understand Guenther's remark when he had said that "...if there are any survivors, they should not even try to get back to Germany."

It was because the whole crew was believed to be cowards for not having destroyed the coding machine and the codebook. And if anybody had returned to Germany he certainly would not make his presence known more than absolutely necessary, at least not for a few years.

I left Hammer's big, yellow house. I noticed the two large aspen trees in the front yard, which had shed all their leaves. A few days earlier the leaves had covered the ground with a beautiful golden carpet. But now the November drizzle had changed everything into a soggy brown mess. Somebody had started a fire, trying to burn leaves. It still smoldered, filling the air with a motionless, bluish cloud of acrid smoke.

I just about made it to our house when the clouds opened fully and the rain started to pour down in buckets.

CHAPTER 33

Should I tell Signe? This question went through my mind all week long. If I told her, I knew she would relapse, would believe that he was alive, would constantly think of him. That would be the end of our relationship.

But, if I did not tell her that I had heard these rumors and reports, it would be a kind of betrayal of her trust. One day she would find out anyway and I would feel horribly, and that would end our relationship too.

She had been good to me, and the nights at the " Vier Jahreszeiten " had been superlative, that's all I could say. She made it easy on me and did not let me know that I had practically no money and that she had to foot most of the bills.

Was I a fool? Shouldn't I leave things as they were?

No, I had to tell her everything.

The next time she came to Hamburg we had dinner together as usual. We went to see a movie and then went back to the hotel.

She showed that she knew me pretty well. She put her arms on the table, supporting her chin and looked at me intensively with a half-smile on her face.

"Dietz, something is on your mind. Please tell me."

I told her what had happened at the funeral and about the meeting with Commodore von Kronebach. And I told her that he was sure that Wolf had survived, that he had been in a POW camp and then escaped to Canada. I also told her about the gentlemen at the reception, who described the feelings of the navy officers and what they believed had happened to their modified coding machines, about the breakdown of the submarine warfare. They all seemed to blame Captain Unger, Ensign Rohrbach and the whole crew for not having destroyed the coding equipment in time.

If Wolf knew about that, or suspected it, and the fact that he was believed to be a "mutineer", would that not have been enough reason for him not to come back to Germany? The more so if he knew that his parents were killed?

I was surprised that Signe did not say one word for a good while. We found a good show on TV, enjoyed it and later on, after making love, we fell asleep.

Suddenly I woke up. Signe's night table light was on. She was sitting up in bed, turning her head from right to left again and again. She was crying.

"Dietz, I know it now! He is alive! Besides what you told me tonight I read a report about German prisoners in America, that nobody ever escaped successfully except two men. One went to Mexico and then back to Germany. The other one escaped from a prison camp in Ohio and wound up in Canada. That is Wolf! I know it, yes!

"I have to go and find him! He might be injured or have some brain damage and not know how to...no, that is nonsense. He might just not want to go back to Germany for those reasons you talked about. I will travel to the USA and Canada, I will find him!"

Then she turned toward me. "I am sorry, Dietz. I tried, both of us tried. But I know now what to do. I love you, yes, but Wolf - he is something really big, powerful. He had been on my mind every day since I last saw him. He is with me day or night. Sorry, but it is that way. I tried to forget him, but I never could."

She now had turned fully toward me and looked at me with bewildered eyes.

"Dietz, please, try to understand!"

It was as if somebody had poured burning coals over me. What did she do to me! This was the second time! Damnit!

"Dietz, - oh, Dietz!"

Signe was sobbing loudly. Her hair was completely dishevelled. What did I care at this time.

Finally I found some words, stammering something like, "Signe... damnit! Are you sure you know what you are doing?"

"Yes, Dietz, I do know."

I knew I could not stop her. I did not want to either. I got dressed and left without saying another word. Don't lose your temper, Dietz, don't!

I was lucky to catch the last train to our suburb.

I was not going to die over this. Now I had lost her twice to Wolf. I knew also that one day I was going to see how stupid I was to try the second time. All I wanted now was to forget her. Period.

I concentrated on my studies and on the practical courses. Then we went through the final examination period and actually wound up in one of the top groups.

The following year I received my papers and immigrated to the United States. Would they accept me, a German, about whom they did not know anything? He might have been an ardent Nazi!

No problem. I had only a few situations where I felt I was not welcome. Later on a few physicians made me feel. unwanted . . Forget about it.

A long period of additional training and further examinations ensued. It was made so much easier by the fact that I had found Ann. I met her in a hospital in Westchester County, where I was an intern. Her friendly smiling Irish eyes and her beauty as well as her appearance of "class" made me fall in love with her. We got married and she followed me without complaining through the years, as I had to take additional training in this city or another.

Yes, she had class and standards. I knew I never would ask her to do anything which basically was not right. This was not even discussed; it was self-understood.

Later on I opened my own practice. I built my own office, was my own boss and felt independent to a degree I had never imagined. Life was extremely busy, and success had come.

In 1972 I managed to find a colleague, who would cover me, and we went for a vacation in California. We had found a golf resort in San Bernardo and were looking forward to ten days of golfing, traveling around San Diego, good food and - sleep. Life was tough, but rewarding. Our children had entered college or were about to do so. Our boy, though, had left college and was traveling with a rock band. He was an excellent lead guitarist. We had an agreement that he would return in a year or two and then continue with college.

I had been able to forget most of the bad things I had seen during the war. Occasionally I must have had bad dreams. Ann would tell me the next morning that I had moaned and groaned and spoken in German. But that had become less and less frequent as the years passed.

I had taken Ann to the first tee. She was going to play in a tournament, substituting for a lady who suddenly had fallen ill. The pro had given her a few lessons before and had suggested her as a replacement -- quite an honor. I myself was going to eat lunch and then write letters and call the office.

I entered the cafeteria and waited to be shown to a seat. I did not see many guests in the room, except a pretty loud group of eight or nine people in one corner. Much laughter came from that direction.

I had barely sat down when all the laughing stopped abruptly. Chairs were pushed back hurriedly, and people jumped to their feet.

Everybody was looking at one lady. She had grasped her throat with one hand and was shaking the other arm wildly. I jumped up too. Was she having a heart attack? Or did she swallow something and it got stuck in her throat?

I pushed my chair away and ran over to her. On her plate was a steak with a large bite taken out of it.

The lady was fighting for air, already turning blue.

"Permit me - I am a doctor."

I worked myself behind her, put my arms around her lower chest, locked my hands, and gave her a few fast compressions. She moved her other hand to her throat, did something like spitting, and a chunk of meat popped out. She heaved a long gasping breath, and then another one.

Her eyes filled with relief. She nodded, indicating that she was all right. Then she panted huskily, "Thank God you were here, Doctor. Thank you ever so much!"

I watched her closely. She seemed to be okay. Her husband grabbed my hands, shaking them. "Doc, thank you, thank you, God bless you!"

Some of the other people got up and did the same. The good old Heimlich maneuver, I said to myself, it works so well.

I felt good. I had one of those very rewarding moments, one you would not want to miss in your life as a doctor.

Somebody had called an ambulance, and we decided it was better to have her checked at the hospital, take chest x-rays and so on.

I sat down and waited for the waitress to come.

While I was waiting I noticed one member of the group staring at me. He was a tall man with dark hair and a few grayish patches at his temples.

I looked again. This man looked somehow familiar to me. Who was it?

He started to walk towards me, slowly, as if he was not quite sure about what he was doing. I noticed the gait, though, immediately: the gait of a panther. I also noticed the wrinkles in his face like his father had them - that was not Wolf Rohrbach, was it? Did I see a ghost?

The man stood now in front of me. He started to say something, but he only stammered:

"Dietz Heller, is that you? Dietz?"

"Wolf Rohrbach! Oh my God! I thought you were...."

"I don't blame you, I know."

The next few minutes were lost in futile attempts to grasp reality. both of us were shaking, stammering.

Finally I got him to sit down and we ordered drinks, still having difficulties in recovering.

"Dietz, for heavens sake, what are you doing here? Are you here by yourself, or with your family? On vacation? Where do you live? What are you doing?"

There were so many questions. And I had even more.

"Wolf - how Wolf, are you here on business? Do you have family with you...?"

We settled down a little.

He said that he was here with a group of Canadian friends, but was leaving early in the morning with his wife to go to Singapore, where he was to open an office for his electronics business. His wife was in San Diego with a friend, and they were not expected to come back until late tonight.

"Your wife - then Signe did meet up with you?"

I wished I had not said that. He shrank away as if in great pain. His voice became husky as he answered.

"I don't really blame you, Dietz, for assuming that," he said. He was on the verge of tears.

"No, Signe - Signe is dead. She died in a shipwreck years ago."

I did not feel anything within myself, not even shock. Just the numbness I had noticed at that time, when I had told her about Wolf's fate.

Had I become feelingless, had I lost all compassion? Dietz, she did not deserve a fate like that, no matter what!

Wolf continued.

"She died in a shipwreck on the way over to find me. She was on a Swedish freighter. It took on a lot of water in a severe storm when the cargo shifted...."

"I am sorry, Wolf, I really am. I don't know what to say."

I realized that I had put my hand on his, and then in turn he covered my hand with his. We sat there in silence for a while. Then he took a deep breath, took his hand off mine, straightened out and sat upright, looking to a point far away.

"Dietz, it was a great loss for me, and it took a few years to get over it.

"How I found out? I was living by then in Canada. Since the first day of my escape I tried everything to contact my family and Signe, tried to tell them that I was alive. That was the main reason why I had to leave the POW camp; they had quarantined us completely, and we were not allowed to contact anybody.

As soon as I got to Canada I tried to write home and to Signe's parents in Sweden.

"No answer. There was no answer from anybody I tried to contact. Finally I wrote to the Swedish Embassy. They wrote back stating in a few words that Signe had been a passenger on a Swedish freighter and that the ship was lost in a hurricane. They gave me a very short report of the sinking. As the last radio message said that the waves were over thirty-five feet high. Yes, it was the tail end of a hurricane.

"By then I had made plans not to go back to Germany, stay somewhere here, maybe in Vancouver, and work myself back to Asia, Singapore, maybe have Signe come over here and marry me...I know, friend, all this is hard to swallow for you, since you yourself were so much interested in her. Damn, it all is so complicated.

"But for her to come over here on her own, not even knowing where I was, whether I was alive or not...it is so hard to say, but don't you think... that she really was going for me? That she wanted me?"

Again he was honest, brutally honest, and he was right. With him still alive, it never would have worked.

But then we had been sure at that time that he was dead, that he was only a memory for both of us, Signe and me, for each one in their own way.

I shook these now useless thoughts off.

"Wolf, you knew about your parents?"

"Yes, I found out about them. I finally remembered my aunt's address and I somehow got through to her. Nobody in Hamburg answered my letters.

"It took a long time for the mail to function again normally."

"Wolf, you went through a lot. But I wish we would have heard from you somehow."

"Dietz, a few more things happened that might explain things to you better. As you might have guessed by now, the submarine was captured, including the whole crew. We had been hit by depth charges and suffered complete loss of control of the sub. There were explosions and then gas, first sulfuric smelling gas, then chlorine gas. We had a vicious fire blocking the radio room, where the coding equipment was, and we could not get to it, as hard as we tried. We could not see or breathe. I heard the captain yell "Abandon ship!" Whoever could scrambled for the ladders and fought his way out. I had tried once more for the coding room to get the enigma, but a large sheet of flames almost got me. I had to give up and finally pulled myself on deck.

"First I hardly could see, but then I noticed several boats with Allied sailors, with gas masks and fire fighting equipment. They forced their way inside and after a few minutes came out with the enigma machine and the code books. Pretty courageous, since they did not know whether we had planted explosives to scuttle the boat.

"Other allied navy men watched us with submachine guns aimed at us. We had no way of fighting, we had no weapons. Finally they brought us on one of their ships .The men of the commando had jumped into their dinghy and left our U-boat. We had a last look at it. Smoke was pouring out of the hatch, and one sailor hung lifeless over the railing. Suddenly a loud explosion rocked our submarine. But it did not sink.

I knew it was over, that is the submarine war. Up to now in the last months the Allies apparently were not able to break our code anymore after we had introduced the fourth rotor, and everybody started to relax a bit. Within a few weeks now,though, they had cracked the code and our losses skyrocketed. Finally Admiral Doenitz had to recall most of the boats, and the Allies had won the battle of the Atlantic. And we had the feeling that we would be blamed for this, Captain Unger and me.

"Dietz, I do have to tell you also what actually happened on the 'Piranha', and why I was transferred.

"One day we had sunk a little freighter with gunfire. There were two lifeboats, apparently in good condition. The freighter's crew seemed to be relatively safe and would make it to shore, which was not that far away. Suddenly von Kronebach stuck his head out of the conning tower and yelled to me, "Ensign Rohrbach, shoot those bastards! Both boats! Those guys are just Chinese coolies!"

"Well, I could not believe what he had ordered. That would be plain murder. I could not help myself but pushed the gunner away and emptied the magazine into the water, aiming somewhere else.

"I believe von Kronebach would have liked to shoot me right there and then, but suddenly the alarm sounded. Airplanes! We ran inside the hatch, the boat had started a crash dive already.

"Years later I found out that we had been branded cowards for not destroying the coding machine, and I had been labeled a mutineer for refusing the commander's orders - enough reason to make me not wanting to go back to Germany. Those guys did not even know what really had been going on!"

"Wolf, do you know that Guenther Hammer died at Harbor Hospital a few years afterwards? He had a brain tumor. He is the one who first told me about your fight with von Kronebach."

""Dietz, let us go outside. It is so stuffy in here."

We went out to the patio to enjoy the great California sunshine. The waitress brought us some more drinks.

In the distance we saw big grayish clouds billowing over a hill. We heard fire sirens. It must have been a brush fire.

Wolf resumed his tale. "You might remember the 'Doenitz order' from those years: you were not to rescue any survivors of ship wrecks ,if that would expose you to great danger, but you also were not to kill them deliberately. Well, in a way I did commit mutiny by not following von Kronebachs orders,--but I followed Doenitzs orders- - So, I believe Guenther Hammer talked the commander into transferring me to Unger's boat to avoid a real showdown between me and von Kronebach. You know what happened then."

Wolf lit a cigarette and then blew the smoke slowly towards the golf course. There was no need for a fast answer. Both of us were sitting there, each one lost in their own thoughts.

But then I remembered one more question I wanted to have answered.

"How did you get out of the camp, Wolf? Heck, that must have been difficult!"

"It was not so complicated. Our prison camp was in Northern Ohio. I could hear trains go by day and night, actually not too far away. I decided if I could get on a train, ride the trains like a hobo for a while, constantly moving from one location to another, they might not get me.

"On a foggy day I managed to escape from a van which had taken some of us prisoners to Toledo. The driver had lost control of it when he could not see the road anymore. I tell you, a November fog in Northern Ohio is quite an experience. You would not believe how thick the fog can be. The van hit a tree and the backdoor sprung open. I got away, found a train soon and rode the rails for a few weeks. I stole food and clothes, something to wear instead of my POW garb. I slept in freight cars. The police were right behind me many times.

"I met a good number of guys on the trains. Some of them were draft dodgers, or escaped prisoners, or just professional hobos. I told them that I was a sailor and did not want to go on the Atlantic any more, I had my fill with the U-boats. They seemed to believe me. You know, I played up my British accent. They gave me the nickname "Liverpool Boy."

"Then I went to Vancouver, and worked for a boss who shipped heating oil all over the West Coast, taking his share of every barrel and making out very well, if you know what I mean. I found out that he protected me in a way, apparently suspecting that I was an escaped POW. He had a German wife and was a German sympathizer.

". . . to wind it up: after the war was over I found an old friend of my father's in Vancouver. I told him my story. He took me under his wings and taught me all about the electronics business. He got me false papers, and they still are good. Don't tell anybody!" Wolf laughed.

"Man," he continued, "I have told you a lot. Now, please, let me know what you did!"

I made it as short as I could. I told him about my time in France and then in Russia, told him about the cruelties I had seen and the stupidity of some of the military leaders. I also mentioned my emotional outburst when I was with the infantry, mentioned what I saw in Branitz and what Hans Wanger had told me and what the SS man had revealed to me.

I also told him what the Germans were thinking after the war, and the only partially successful denazification program. I could not avoid telling the story of my brother's death and what happened to the penicillin that his teacher had obtained from Switzerland.

"Dietz, I understand you. I am happy you made it out of there. I have not seen any hope for me in Germany and I tell you why: I knew I was considered to be a mutineer, and I knew that I was a despised man after we had not been able to destroy the code machine. At one time I made a few phone calls to Germany. Your phone was out, so were many others yet. But I made connection with one of my navy friends, a comrade from the submarine school. He refused to talk with me and had his wife tell me that I was a dead man to the whole submarine corps because of my so-called mutiny and because of the coding machine. I should never again try to contact him or anybody who was in the submarine corps.

"What happened to this guy, who was a good friend of mine for years? Dietz, if this spirit will remain in Germany, or maybe even would be rekindled - no, I don't think this will happen. People will have learned by now. I hope so.

"I believe they will get over it and channel their energy in other directions, like trade.

"But I don't want to wait that long. I feel insecure about life in Germany. I'd rather stay here or in the Far East. I have a good wife, two beautiful children and I love our home in Vancouver. My business is doing well. Remember that I told you years ago that I would not mind going back to Asia?"

"Yes, I remember that. It is strange, though, isn't it, that both of us have left Germany, for pretty similar reasons. I am happy here, and from what I can read from your tale, you are satisfied too. It is so good to see you."

Wolf looked now rather exhausted.

"Dietz, excuse me, but I cannot talk much any more. I wish you could meet Maureen, and I wish I could see Ann. Maureen will come back late from San Diego, and we have to catch an early flight to L.A. to go to Singapore. But we will get together somehow, sometime. Here is my card."

We exchanged cards.

"By the way, what you did in the cafeteria was just unbelievable. Well, good luck and Tschuess!" We shook hands.

As he walked towards the door I noted that he was bent over at first. Then he straightened up as if he had received a shot of some secret, powerful medicine. Did I hear him whistle? Yes, and it was his favorite song from many years ago, "Jeepers-creepers!"

Then I knew he would get over his horrible experiences - one of these days he hopefully would forget.

I finished my cigarette, crushed it in the ashtray and went up to my room.

CHAPTER 34

Ann came back from her golf game, and she was in good spirits and very happy. She had played well and their team had made second. When I told her my story about meeting and talking with Wolf, she listened with initial disbelief. After a while, though, she started to cry when I described to her how Wolf had been so depressed when he talked about Signe and the death of his parents, and the treatment he received from his old "friends". Ann knew about our affair with Signe. She felt a little better when I told her about "Jeepers-creepers" and how Wolf then apparently recovered.

"That must have been really hard on him. But Dietz, I know from my studies in psychology that it might have a good effect on him to have talked about these events with you, who certainly could understand his experiences well. Maybe he will call in a few weeks, wanting to talk more. Let's hope it will work that way."

The same night I had a nightmare. I dreamt that I was back in Russia in the three-man bunker, and then in Branitz Hospital. Hans Wanger appeared in that dream and said, "If you ever have a chance to get out of Europe, take it. One of these days you will know why I say this!"

Later I must have found easier sleep, because when I woke up I felt relaxed and refreshed. At last I had found the answer to all the questions that had surrounded Wolf's fate - and Signe's, as sad as hers was.

Ann and I returned to our hometown in the Midwest. A great deal of work was waiting. I did not have much time to think about California and the meeting with Wolf. Ann was busy getting our youngest daughter ready for college. Life was as before, with quite a few night calls and emergency surgeries.

After about three weeks I took a break and signed out for the evening to a colleague. We were going to join a birthday party at the club.

I poured myself a drink and stepped outside onto the patio. A steady, warm, westerly breeze blew in from Lake Erie and made the pine trees rustle. Over at the marina it caused a rhythmical clanging as the shoots of the sailboats hit the metal masts.

I always liked listening to the sound of wind going through trees, whether it was years ago as a child standing at the Elbe River or later in the black Forest or in Arcachon. A mild wind blew also at the shores of the Baltic Sea at night. I could see some flashing lights at the horizon, and a distant rumble came across the water. Was it thunder and lightning, or did the navy have gun practice?

As I stood there, lost in my thoughts, I heard a tune welling up in my mind - not completely unexpected.

"Yes, I will find the Golden River. . . "

Sure, it was my old battle cry, which had been with me for so many years, my song of defiance, adventure and the longing for independence and freedom. With a lot of luck I had "crossed the mountains" and had found this metaphoric river, that is the treasure of a worthwhile life in freedom.

I had to think of the men I had met, like Lieutenant LeClaire, Georg Osten and Karl Weber, and the Silesian guys with Corporal Konjetzny. And Roland Horn - what ever happened to him? When we were in Berlin a few years ago I tried to find Karl Weber, but I did not have any success. And Hans Wanger! Did he every make it to Canada?

Ann came out of the house with a glass of wine and joined me.

I put my arm around her, and both of us looked over Lake Erie. The afternoon sun had turned the clouds red and golden. As we stood there a large sailboat glided silently out of the harbor. The crew hoisted the jib and it fluttered in the wind for a few seconds until the crew tightened the line. Then they raised the mainsail. The boat heeled over a little and gained speed fast.

Finally we tore ourselves away from this view and went inside to get dressed. The wonderful, warm breeze made us close only the screen door.

We were thankful, and it was good to be alive. Yes, there would be years of struggling and there would be some crises, but we felt deeply that we were on our way.

EPILOGUE

This is the story I wanted to tell you. No, Wolf and I have not met again, at least not so far. Maybe Signe's shadow hung too much over our relationship. I still admire Wolf for what he did on the submarine, when he stopped the cannon.

For me it is enough to know that I did what I thought I had to do, and I am happy that I had a chance to succeed. Wolf also had acted the way his beliefs made him, and he seemed to be satisfied with his life. Both of us had prevailed in our fight against excessive militarism and the Nazis, and he had successfully fought against obvious cruelty.

Well, that's all I have to tell. Let me check what I wrote, print it and then shut off the computer.